LEGAL PRACTICE HANDBOOK

ADVOCACY

Avrom Sherr
Professor of Law
Centre for Business and Professional Law,
University of Liverpool

Series Editor: Anthony G. King, MA, Solicitor
Director of Education, Clifford Chance

BLACKSTONE
PRESS LIMITED

First published in Great Britain 1993 by Blackstone Press Limited,
9-15 Aldine Street, London W12 8AW. Telephone 081-740 1173

© Avrom Sherr, 1993

ISBN: 1 85431 172 7

British Library Cataloguing in Publication Data
A CIP catalogue record for this book is available from the British
Library

Typeset by Montage Studios Limited, Tonbridge, Kent
Printed by BPCC Wheatons Ltd, Exeter

Contents

Preface

I have been teaching advocacy for so many years now that it is difficult to remember how many of the ideas mentioned in this book are original and how many derive clearly or solely from other sources. I know that I am entirely indebted to two other people for many of the ideas, or the confirmation of them. Roger Burridge at Warwick University and Paul Bergman at UCLA (two outstanding advocates and teachers) sat together for two hours one wintry afternoon whilst Paul was visiting Warwick in the early 1980s. Those two hilarious hours have already spawned two articles on the subject and were certainly among the generative beginnings of this book (and perhaps also elements of Paul Bergman's latest editions of *Trial Advocacy*). Many of the ideas were common to the three of us and some definitely emanated from the other two. My indebtedness to them for those ideas is set out clearly here and also to the thousands of law students, lawyers, health and safety inspectors, social workers and others who have been involved in my advocacy courses over the years. Thank are also due to Tony King, Glenn Brasse and Rod Morgan for careful comments on an earlier draft and especially to Sheila Wood for painstaking typing. All of them have enriched the text somewhat, though any faults are entirely those of Bergman and Burridge.

Avrom Sherr
Alsop Wilkinson Professor of Law
Centre for Business and Professional Law
Faculty of Law, University of Liverpool
July 1993

Dedication

This book is dedicated to Liora Tamar Sara Sherr during whose gestation it was conceived and written. The first draft of the book was concluded on the day of her birth, 22 January 1993.

Introduction: New Advocacy Roles and Skills Standards

This book is intended as an introduction to the skills of advocacy. It is written both for new and less experienced advocates as well as for those involved in training them. Unlike the traditional texts on advocacy it is not replete with witty war stories having the appearance of being so much better in the repetition than in their likely occurrence. Neither will it provide a neatly alliterative set of clever catechisms covering credibiity in court.

Rather, its aim is to set out simply and clearly the basics of the art and science of advocacy and the means of practising the basic skills both inside and outside of the court, tribunal or other forum.

As a pervasive concept in the background to this text advocacy is seen as a wider occurrence than the specifically formal ritual of the courtroom, tribunal or arbitration forum. Advocacy of an idea, an opinion or an argument is something known to all social beings and is an integral part of general social interaction. It occurs certainly within the lawyer's office both over the telephone and in meetings with 'the other side' as a part of the process normally known as negotiation. It occurs in lawyers' offices as lawyers take clients through alternative proposals for dealing with their case. Advocacy occurs between lawyers during internal meetings inside firms to decide how the firm is to be run, whether there should be computers on lawyers' desks, whether more trainee solicitors should be taken on and whether a new photocopier should be purchased.

Advocacy also occurs between individuals deciding on which film to see, which restaurant to go to, what holiday to take this year and whether to buy a new compact disc player. Although this book is confined strictly to the work of advocacy within law, it builds on the existing social skills possessed by new advocates but perhaps not naturally visualised as appropriate for the cut and thrust of trial.

Breaking one of its own rules for the new advocate, the book takes for granted a basic understanding of the legal process and the nature of the practice of law. It addresses young lawyers who possess some background and now wish to venture into advocacy.

This book also accentuates the 'tip of the iceberg' nature of forensic advocacy, in its marginal significance in relation to the work of preparation for the forensic event. The bulk of the competent advocate's work is not carried out on the advocate's feet on the day of the hearing, but in the long days and nights beforehand ensuring that all of the law and procedure is understood, all arguments are covered, all evidence is ready and techniques of persuasion are well-practised and at hand. Good advocacy is not *creatio ex nihilo*, or the deity creating a world out of chaos, but merely the icing and cherry on the well-baked ingredients of a carefully prepared cake.

The skills of advocacy will now be an essential part of each qualified solicitor's repertoire as well as that of the barrister. The Council for Legal Education's vocational course now involves full advocacy training for barristers. It is the Law Society's confirmed intention that rights of advocacy for solicitors will be extended within the early 1990s. Together with such extension of rights comes the responsibility to ensure that all aspiring advocates are properly trained and grounded in the basic skills.

In order to ensure that new generations of solicitors will be adequately prepared for their new role, the Law Society has devised three sets of skills standards in advocacy training to be achieved through:

(a)   the Legal Practice Course (the new Law Society final examination) starting in September 1993;

(b)   the Professional Skills Course to be taken during articles, starting in September 1994;

(c)   the training contract, or period of articles itself, and the informal or formal, on-the-job training during articles.

Although some of these standards are not yet in final, approved form, they are presented here for guidance as to what is likely to be necessary at each stage. These standards will be published by the Law Society in due course. In their three constituent parts, some necessary repetition exists. They are presented here as drafted so that an advocate or trainer may be aware of what is expected separately at each stage. They are also useful, in general as a guide to what might be expected of a new advocate.

The foundation training will take place in the Legal Practice Course.

Draft skills standards on advocacy in the Legal Practice Course

The student should be able to formulate a coherent submission based upon facts, general principles and legal authority in a structured, concise and persuasive manner. The student should understand the crucial importance of preparation and the best way to undertake it. The student should be able to demonstrate an understanding of the basic skills in the presentation of cases before various courts and tribunals and should be able to:

(a)   identify the client's goals;

(b)   identify and analyse factual material;

(c)   identify the legal context in which factual issues arise;

(d)   relate the central legal and factual issues to each other;

(e)   state in summary form the strengths and weaknesses of the case from each party's perspective;

(f)   develop a case presentation strategy;

(g)   outline the facts in simple narrative form;

(h)   prepare in simple form the legal framework for the case;

(i)   prepare the submission as a series of propositions based on the evidence;

(j)   identify, analyse and assess the specific communication skills and techniques employed by the presenting advocate;

(k)   demonstrate an understanding of the purpose, techniques and tactics of examination, cross-examination and re-examination to adduce, rebut and clarify evidence;

(l)   demonstrate an understanding of the ethics, etiquette and conventions of advocacy.

It is assumed that the student should already have developed oral and written communication skills, interpersonal skills, and the skills of legal analysis and research. It is assumed, in particular, that a student should be able to:

(a)   listen effectively;

(b)   engage in oral discussion in a clear and concise fashion;

(c)   record or summarise a discussion in clear and concise notes;

(d)   write clearly and precisely with attention to grammar, style organisation, bibliographies and citations;

(e)   work cooperatively with others in small groups;

(f)   extract, analyse and apply up-to-date law from primary sources, including case reports, primary and delegated legislation.

In addiition to the skills learned in the legal practice course, trainee solicitors will be taught further skills during their articles in a five-day course, as part of the professional skills course.

Draft skills standards on advocacy and oral communication to be addressed in the Professional Skills Course taken during the training contract (articles)

On completion of the advocacy unit trainees should be competent to exercise the rights of audience available on admission.

It is assumed that as a consequence of the Legal Practice Course trainees will already be able to:

(a)   interview a client;

(b)   identify the client's goals;

(c)   identify and analyse factual material;

(d)   identify the legal context in which factual issues arise;

(e)   relate the central legal and factual issues to each other;

(f)   state in summary form the strengths and weaknesses of the case from each party's perspective;

(g)   develop a case presentation strategy;

(h)   outline the facts in simple narrative forms;

(i)   prepare in simple form the legal framework for the case;

(j)   formulate a coherent submission based upon facts, general principles and legal authority in a structured, concise and persuasive manner;

(k)   identify, analyse and assess the specific communication skills and techniques employed by the presenting advocate;

(l)   demonstrate an understanding of the purpose, techniques and tactics of examination, cross-examination and re-examination to adduce, rebut and clarify evidence;

(m) demonstrate an understanding of the ethics, etiquette and conventions of advocacy.

Trainees should, in addition, be able to advise a client on the appropriate pre-trial procedures and proceedings, understand the crucial importance of preparation and the best way to undertake it, and assist in the preparation and conduct of pre-trial procedures and proceedings.

Trainees should be able to make an interlocutory application before a district judge.

On completion of the Professional Skills Course advocacy module trainees should be able to:

(a) exercise rights of audience available on admission;

(b) create the conditions for effective communication with the client, witness(es), other advocates and triers of fact and law;

(c) use language appropriate to the clients, witness(es) and triers of fact and law;

(d) speak and question effectively;

(e) use a variety of presentation skills to open and close a case;

(f) use a variety of questioning skills to conduct examination-in-chief, cross-examination, and re-examination;

(g) listen, observe and interpret the behaviour of triers of fact and law, client, witness(es) and other advocates and be able to respond to this behaviour as appropriate;

(h) prepare a witness for examination and cross-examination;

(i) present a coherent submission based upon facts, general principles and legal authority in a structured, concise and persuasive manner;

(j) present a submission as a series of propositions based on the evidence;

(k) organise and present evidence in a coherent and organised form;

(l) identify and act upon the ethical problems that arise in the course of a trial.

Trainees should be able to demonstrate these skills in cases or transactions in the criminal courts and the civil courts and in one of the following: family cases, industrial tribunals, planning enquiries, other statutory tribunals, alternative forms of dispute resolution.

Trainees should be able to question a variety of witnesses in the appropriate manner (e.g., expert witnesses, hostile witnesses, biased, untruthful or mistaken witnesses, sympathetic witnesses, and identification witnesses, a witness with previous convictions, a witness who has made a prior admission, child witnesses).

Trainees should consider the interest which the client may have to resolve a dispute by settlement or through forms of alternative dispute resolution rather than by litigation, be able to state the central issues of the case simply to the client and explain the benefits and disadvantages of settlement, and be able to agree suitable action with the client and where appropriate adopt the proper techniques to settle a case.

Apart from these two sets of direct formal teaching, trainees are expected to reinforce skills learned in these courses and develop other skills by learning on the job itself under supervision.

Draft skills standards on advocacy and oral communication to be addressed during the training contract

On completion of the training contract trainees should be competent to exercise the rights of audience available to solicitors on admission. They should have had experience which will enable them to understand the need to use the specific communication skills of the advocate and the techniques and tactics of examination, cross-examination and re-examination. They should understand the need to act in accordance with the ethics, etiquette and conventions of the professional advocate.

During the legal practice course trainees will have been instructed in the general principles involved in advocacy through role plays and simulation. They will, also, have been given instruction on the appropriate pre-trial procedures and proceedings, and through simulation, on how to make interlocutory applications before a district judge.

During the Professional Skills Course trainees will be given experience, through simulation and role play, that will enable them to:

    (a)   use the specific communication skills and techniques employed by the presenting advocate;

    (b)   demonstrate the techniques and tactics of examination, cross-examination and re-examination to adduce, rebut and clarify evidence;

    (c)   act in accordance with the ethics, etiquette and conventions of the professional advocate.

During the training contract trainees should be given practical opportunities that will enable them to understand the principles involved in preparing, conducting and presenting a case, including the need to:

    (a)   identify the client's goals;

    (b)   identify and analyse relevant factual and legal issues and relate them to one another;

    (c)   summarise the strengths and weaknesses of each party's case;

    (d)   plan how to present the case;

(e)   outline the facts in simple narrative form;

(f)   formulate a coherent submission based upon facts, general principles and legal authority in a structured, concise and persuasive manner.

To help trainees develop these skills they could:

(a)   help advise on pre-trial procedures;

(b)   help prepare cases before trial;

(c)   in the company of one or more lawyers, attend a magistrates' court to observe trials, bail applications, pleas of mitigation or committal;

(d)   observe the conduct of a submission in chambers or examination, cross-examination and re-examination in open court;

(e)   observe proceedings in family cases, industrial tribunals, planning tribunals or other statutory tribunals or the use of alternative forums of dispute resolution; or

(f)   as training progresses, and under appropriate supervision, take a more active role in the conduct of a case. This could include interlocutory applications before a master or district judge.

Supervisors should discuss the progress of a case with trainees and review with them the performance of advocates. Supervisors should review the trainee's own performance, drawing attention to those aspects which could be improved.

Through this threefold approach future generations of trainee solicitors will be far better prepared than their predecessors for their new advocacy role. These standards have been published here verbatim. It should be noted that they are *not* yet final, although it is unlikely that they will be subject to major changes.

It will be seen that there is a concentration on the formally taught elements of the Legal Practice Course and Professional Skills Course and the standards to be achieved as a result of the work experience of articles is rather more vague. This is intended to deal with the wide variations in work to be found in different firms.

Although it is clear that many solicitors, and especially those in particular types of law firms, are unlikely to wish to practise their skills often within the forensic setting, there are still enormous advantages in learning the practice of the advocate. All those who prepare litigation cases as solicitors, and all those who advise others in all fields of law where litigation may arise at a later date are given an enormous benefit when they understand how a case proceeds in court. Advising clients on a daily basis is strengthened and enhanced by the ultimate knowledge of how a case, if needs be, might be presented and how it might be accepted at trial. Rather than leading lawyers to be more risk averse as a result of this knowledge it can provide a strength of action in appropriate circumstances, impetus to negotiate in others and simple understanding of the necessities of the courtroom for those preparing cases.

Though this book will emphasise the importance of proper representation, it clearly cannot deal with the entire range of all legal skills involving client interviewing and counselling, legal and factual investigation, drafting and negotiation, etc. The book therefore opens with an introduction to these issues and their importance, the details of which need to be derived from elsewhere. Other books in the Legal Practice Handbook series should be helpful in providing both background and detail for these areas. The overall structure of most hearings is then presented and the book is then divided up in accordance with the structure of a hearing. It concentrates on each aspect of the hearing in turn and the differential skills involved in each.

In relation to each of these subdivisions the specific skills are portrayed together with some suggestions for examples of exercises which might be used in an advocacy training course. These exercises are intended as illustrations of the skills described and are intended to be as useful to the reader as to someone involved in a course.

Accordingly they are written within the continuous prose of the text and should be read in that way.

An introductory text of this nature is not able to cover extended areas of advocacy. Little will be mentioned on higher-level appellate hearings and the nature of argument and advocacy there, although many of the ideas addressed will be relevant. Similarly, the particular problems of a jury trial, insofar as persuading a jury is different from persuading magistrates or a judge, are not specifically covered but once again most of what is here will be relevant.

The text also assumes a basic understanding of general court process to the level which should be achieved during the Law Society Finals, Legal Practice Course or Bar Vocational Course. Law undergraduates would usually have achieved this basic level of understanding as a result of a Legal Method or Legal System Course. The detailed process of any one court or tribunal is not assumed, or addressed.

The intention is

(a)   to demystify advocacy,

(b)   to separate advocacy into its constituent parts

and to demonstrate techniques and skills necessary in each.

It is hoped that you will enjoy reading the book and have good fortune and good skills always with you in court!

Chapter One

Advocacy, Oral Communication and Representation

In this chapter the nature of advocacy is addressed by comparing it with the more general concepts of oral communication and representation. The intention is to define the role of advocacy within areas of human behaviour such as social communication which are better known to the new advocate. A large part of the chapter also sets out the barristers' and solicitors' rules of conduct in relation to advocacy. These are essential items for the new advocate to know. However, they are a little indigestible set out in full. The reader should feel free to skip those on a first reading, in order to return to them later.

1.1 ORAL COMMUNICATION

Some basic needs of all oral communication can first be addressed. All oral communication needs to be audible, understandable and appropriate. These are clearly context specific. That is to say, what might be audible in a client conference room may not be audible in a lecture room of a hundred people with air-conditioning units helping to drown out the sound. Also, what might be understandable by an unsophisticated client will be quite different from what might be understandable for a room full of conveyancing lawyers. And what may be appropriate to say to one person or group within a particular setting may be quite distinct from what one might say to the same people in another setting.

General social awareness teaches us most of these skills and it is unlikely that we will speak too loudly in a small room with one other person, that we will address a Women's Institute meeting as 'Gentlemen' and so on. If speaking for the first time at a university seminar it would be normal to wait to hear the expected mode and form of address and the style in which others speak before opening one's mouth. Addressing any larger meeting one would probably try to find out whether it was the norm to address the President, Chair or Chancellor of the Duchy first before the rest of the audience. Speaking after dinner one might make jokes, and they might be more ribald at a single-sex function or within a particular club or group. It would be unusual to make jokes at a funeral or a viva voce examination. The general rule therefore for all oral communication is clearly to sense the appropriateness of the occasion by looking at its prime purpose and to measure one's oral communication against that purpose and setting.

The new Bar final course, taught at the Inns of Court School of Law, contains detailed suggestions on how to improve the projection of one's speech, how to improve breathing and the power of the diaphragm. The exercises suggested come from the world of the theatre. They may well be useful to those advocates who find it difficult to speak sufficiently loudly for the particular legal context in which they will advocate. For most people this will not present a great problem, although a full trial can mean a number of hours on one's feet whilst speaking for a large proportion of the time. Exercises may be helpful to assist anyone with 'a still small voice'.

Interestingly, a sense of what is appropriate in particular social settings seems to come better to the introvert than the so-called 'natural' extrovert advocate. Many lessons can be learned from those with a little more reserve. Perhaps the best rule of thumb with which to start is 'If in doubt, don't say it!'

These skills of oral communication are not dissimilar to those expected under the Law Society's Skills Standards, set out in the Introduction.

1.2   REPRESENTATION

Representing a cause, or putting a specific view is a particular species of oral communication. All of the previous principles relating to oral communication will apply and some more are added.

For example, in order to encourage whoever you are trying to convince it is necessary not simply to inform but also to be believed and to persuade. This means that it is essential not to annoy the person to whom the representation is made and in general to make a case which goes mostly in favour of the view being represented.

It is useful to appear honourable and sensible and sensitive so that the listener does not see you as completely one-sided and unobjective. It is also sensible to gauge the reaction of the listener to the representation in order to make sure of its effectiveness. This is, perhaps, a part of knowing one's audience and appropriate communication, both essential for oral communication in general, but even more important in representing a view or a cause.

A loose tongue, which might be fun in a more general talk, would have to be more closely guarded in representation in order to ensure not only that what is said is appropriate but also that it achieves the overall aim.

1.3   ADVOCACY

Advocacy as practised in formal legal hearings is but a more specific sub-species of oral representation. Once again the same basic principles apply but further principles are added.

The rules of appropriate, audible, understandable speech are equally if not more important. Rules about persuading with honourable objectivity also exist as do care in not pleading the other side's case. The additional rules applying to advocacy can be divided into sets of duties the legal advocate has and the style and formality of representations of an advocate in a legal forum.

1.4 THE ADVOCATE'S DUTIES

1.4.1 Duties to the court

The codes of conduct for solicitors and barristers lay down clear sets of general rules. Although they are a little indigestible in one clump, the more general elements of duty are set out in this chapter, so that they can provide a firm foundation for the skills which follow. The reader anxious to proceed can go straight to 1.4.2, but should return to dip into the professional codes later.

The barristers' code of professional etiquette suggests both broad and detailed principles for the conduct of advocacy. Some are set out here and others will be found at appropriate points later in the text.

610 A practising barrister when conducting proceedings at court:

(a) is personally responsible for the conduct and presentation of his case and must exercise personal judgment upon the substance and purpose of statements made and questions asked;

(b) must not unless invited to do so by the court or when appearing before a tribunal where it is his duty to do so assert a personal opinion of the facts or the law;

(c) must ensure that the court is informed of all relevant decisions and legislative provisions of which he is aware whether the effect is favourable or unfavourable towards the contention for which he argues and must bring any procedural irregularity to the attention of the court during the hearing and not reserve such matter to be raised on appeal;

5.2 A barrister must assist the court in the administration of justice and, as part of this obligation and the obligation to use only proper and lawful means to promote and protect the interests of his client, must not deceive or knowingly or recklessly mislead the court.

5.3 A barrister is at all times individually and personally responsible for his own conduct and for his professional work both in court and out of court.

5.5 A barrister must at all times be courteous to the court and to all those with whom he has professional dealings.

5.11 A barrister must take all reasonable and practicable steps to avoid unnecessary expense or waste of the court's time. He should, when asked, inform the court of the probable length of his case; and he should also inform the court of any developments which affect information already provided.

The Guide to the Professional Conduct of Solicitors sets out some specific principles in relation to the solicitor advocate's duty to the court. Some of the main general obligations are set out in full here and others will appear in the text at appropriate places.

14.01 Principle

A solicitor who acts in litigation, whilst owing a duty to his client to do his best for him, must never deceive or mislead the court.

Commentary

1 Although a solicitor is entitled to take every point, technical or otherwise, that is fairly arguable on behalf of his client, the court must be advised of relevant cases and statutory provisions by the advocates on both sides; if one of them omits a case or provision or makes an incorrect reference to a case or provision, it is the duty of the other to draw attention to it even if it assists his opponent's case.

2 Except when acting or appearing for the prosecution, a solicitor who knows of facts which, or of a witness who, would assist his adversary is not under any duty to inform his adversary or the court of this to the prejudice of his own client. But if the solicitor knows that a relevant affidavit has been filed in the proceedings and is therefore notionally within the knowledge of the court, then his duty is to inform the judge of its existence.

3   A solicitor would be guilty of unbefitting conduct should he call a witness whose evidence is untrue to the solicitor's knowledge, as opposed to his belief.

4   The above principle applies equally to proceedings before tribunals and inquiries as well as to proceedings before the courts.

The solicitor as advocate for the prosecution

14.13   Principle

Whilst a solicitor prosecuting a criminal case must ensure that every material point is made which supports the prosecution, in presenting the evidence he must do so dispassionately and with scrupulous fairness.

Commentary

1   The prosecutor should state all relevant facts and should limit his expressions of opinion to those fairly required to present his case. He should reveal any mitigating circumstances; he should inform the court of its sentencing powers if invited to do so and whenever it appears to be under a misapprehension about those powers.

2   If a prosecutor obtains evidence which he does not intend to use but which may assist the defence, he must supply particulars of witnesses to the defence, but is not obliged to supply copies of the statements made by those witnesses. If, however, he knows of a credible witness who can speak to material facts which tend to show the accused to be innocent, he must either call that witness himself or make his statement available to the defence. Further, if he knows, not of a credible witness but a witness whom he does not accept as credible, he should tell the defence about him so that they can call him if they wish. The prosecutor must reveal to the defence factual evidence of which he has knowledge and which is inconsistent with that which he, as prosecutor, has presented or proposes to present to the court.

3   The prosecutor must reveal all relevant cases and statutory provisions known to him whether it be for or against his case. This is so whether or not he has been called upon to argue the point in question. (See above principle 14.01.)

The Bar's code is similar:

1   Responsibilities of prosecuting counsel

1.1   Prosecuting counsel should not attempt to obtain a conviction by all means at his command. He should not regard himself as appearing for a party. He should lay before the court fairly and impartially the whole of the facts which comprise the case for the prosecution and should assist the court on all matters of law applicable to the case.

1.2   Prosecuting counsel should bear in mind at all times whilst he is instructed that he is responsible for the presentation and general conduct of the case and that it is his duty to ensure that all relevant evidence is either presented by the prosecution or made available to the defence.

The Guide to the Professional Conduct of Solicitors continues:

The solicitor as advocate for the defence

14.14   Principle

A solicitor who appears in court for the defence in a criminal case is under a duty to say on behalf of the client what the client should properly say for himself if he possessed the requisite skill and knowledge. He has a concurrent duty to ensure that the prosecution discharges the onus placed upon it to prove the guilt of the accused.

Commentary

1   Unlike the advocate for the prosecution, a solicitor who appears for the defendant is under no duty of disclosure to the prosecution or the court, save that he is bound to reveal all

relevant cases and statutory provisions. Moreover, save in exceptional and specific circumstances, the client's privilege precludes him from making a disclosure of privileged material without the client's consent. Consequently, he must not, without instructions, disclose facts known to him regarding his client's character or antecedents nor must he correct any information which may be given to the court by the prosecution if the correction would be to his client's detriment. He must not, however, knowingly himself put forward or let his client put forward false information with intent to mislead the court. Similarly, he must not indicate his agreement with information that the prosecution puts forward which he knows to be false. For further guidance, see Appendix C24 (of the *Solicitors Code of Conduct Booklet*).

2   It is an implied term of the advocate's retainer that he is free to present his client's case at the trial or hearing in such a way as he considers appropriate. If the client's express instructions do not permit the solicitor to present the case in a manner which he considers to be the most appropriate, then, unless his instructions are varied, he may withdraw from the case after seeking the approval of the court to that course, but without disclosing matters which are protected by the client's privilege.

3   If the client instructs his solicitor that he is not guilty, the solicitor must put before the court his client's defence, even if the client decides not to give evidence himself and must, in any event, put the prosecution to proof. Whilst a solicitor may present a technical defence which is available to the client, he must never fabricate a defence on the facts.

4   In general, there is no duty upon a solicitor to enquire in every case where he is instructed as to whether the client is telling the truth. However, where his instructions or other information are such as should put him upon enquiry, he must, where practicable check the truth of what the client tells him to the extent that such statements will be relied upon before the court, or in pleadings or affidavits.

5   Where, prior to the commencement or during the course of the proceedings, a client admits to his solicitor that he is guilty of the charge, the solicitor must decline to act in the proceedings if the client insists on giving evidence in the witness-box in denial of guilt or requires the making of a statement asserting his innocence. The advocate who acts for a client who has admitted his guilt but has pleaded not guilty (as he is so entitled) is under a duty to put the prosecution to proof of its case and may submit that there is insufficient evidence to justify a conviction. Further, the advocate may advance any defence open to the client, other than protesting his innocence or suggesting, expressly or by implication, that someone other than the client committed the offence.

6   If, either before or during the course of proceedings, the client makes statements to his solicitor which are inconsistent, this is not of itself a ground for the solicitor to refuse to act further on behalf of the client. Only where it is clear that the client is attempting to put forward false evidence to the court should the solicitor cease to act. In other circumstances, it would be for the court, and not the solicitor, to assess the truth or otherwise of the client's statement.

7   If the client wishes to plead guilty, but at the same time asserts the truth of facts which, if true, would or could lead to an acquittal, the solicitor should use his best endeavours to persuade his client to plead not guilty. However, if the client insists on pleading guilty, despite being advised that such a plea may or will restrict the ambit of any plea in mitigation or appeal, then the solicitor is not prevented from continuing to act in accordance with the client's instructions, doing the best he can. The solicitor will not, in mitigation, be entitled to suggest that the facts are such that the ingredients of the offence have not been established.

The Bar's code is once again similar:

2   Responsibilities of defence counsel

2.1   When defending a client on a criminal charge, a barrister must endeavour to protect his client from conviction except by a competent tribunal and upon legally admissible evidence sufficient to support a conviction for the offence charged.

2.5 Where a defendant tells his counsel that he did not commit the offence with which he is charged but nevertheless insists on pleading guilty to it for reasons of his own, counsel must continue to represent him, but only after he has advised what the consequences will be and that what can be submitted in mitigation can only be on the basis that the client is guilty.

3 Confessions of guilt

3.1 In considering the duty of counsel retained to defend a person charged with an offence who confesses to his counsel that he did commit the offence charged, it is essential to bear the following points clearly in mind:

(a) that every punishable crime is a breach of common or statute law committed by a person of sound mind and understanding;

(b) that the issue in a criminal trial is always whether the defendant is guilty of the offence charged, never whether he is innocent;

(c) that the burden of proof rests on the prosecution.

3.2 It follows that the mere fact that a person charged with a crime has confessed to his counsel that he did commit the offence charged is no bar to that barrister appearing or continuing to appear in his defence, nor indeed does such a confession release the barrister from his imperative duty to do all that he honourably can for his client.

3.3 Such a confession, however, imposes very strict limitations on the conduct of the defence. A barrister must not assert as true that which he knows to be false. He must not connive at, much less attempt to substantiate, a fraud.

3.4   While, therefore, it would be right to take any objections to the competency of the court, to the form of the indictment, to the admissibility of any evidence or to the evidence admitted, it would be wrong to suggest that some other person had committed the offence charged, or to call any evidence which the barrister must know to be false having regard to the confession, such, for instance, as evidence in support of an alibi. In other words, a barrister must not (whether called by the defendant or otherwise) set up an affirmative case inconsistent with the confession made to him.

3.5   A more difficult question is within what limits may counsel attack the evidence for the prosecution either by cross-examination or in his speech to the tribunal charged with the decision of the facts. No clearer rule can be laid down than this; that he is entitled to test the evidence given by each individual witness and to argue that the evidence taken as a whole is insufficient to amount to proof that the defendant is guilty of the offence charged. Further than this he ought not to go.

3.6   The foregoing is based on the assumption that the defendant has made a clear confession that he did commit the offence charged, and does not profess to deal with the very difficult questions which may present themselves to a barrister when a series of inconsistent statements are made to him by the defendant before or during the proceedings; nor does it deal with the questions which may arise where statements are made by the defendant which point almost irresistibly to the conclusion that the defendant is guilty but do not amount to a clear confession. Statements of this kind may inhibit the defence, but questions arising on them can only be answered after careful consideration of the actual circumstances of the particular case.

The Guide to the Professional Conduct of Solicitors continues:

Solicitor acting as advocate in civil proceedings

14.15   Principle

A solicitor who appears in court or in chambers in civil proceedings is under a duty to say on behalf of the client what the client should properly say for himself if he possessed the requisite skill and knowledge.

Commentary

1   A solicitor who appears as advocate for the plaintiff, the defendant or any other party in civil proceedings is under no duty of disclosure to the other parties or the court, save that he is bound to reveal all relevant cases and statutory provisions. (However, care should be taken here, as the general rules of discovery have effect along with aspects of the Matrimonial Causes Rules asking for full and frank disclosure.) Moreover, save in exceptional and specific circumstances, the client's privilege precludes him from making a disclosure of privileged material without the client's consent. However, the advocate should not act in such a way that, in the context of the language used by him, his failure to disclose amounts to a positive deception of the court.

2   It is an implied term of the advocate's retainer that he is free to present his client's case at the trial or hearing in such a way as he considers appropriate. If the client's express instructions do not permit the solicitor to present the case in what he considers to be the most appropriate manner, then unless his instructions are varied, he may withdraw from the case after seeking the approval of the court to that course, but without disclosing matters which are protected by the client's privilege.

3   Whilst a solicitor may present any technical argument which is available to the client, he must never fabricate an argument on the facts for his client.

4   In general, there is no duty upon a solicitor to enquire in every case where he is instructed as to whether the client is telling the truth. However, where the solicitor's instructions or other information are such as should put him upon enquiry, a solicitor must, where practicable, check the truth of what the client tells him to the extent that such statements will be relied on before the court or in pleadings or affidavits.

5   If, either before or during the course of proceedings, the client makes statements to his solicitor which are inconsistent, this is not of itself a ground for the solicitor to refuse to act further on behalf of the client. Only where it is clear that the client is attempting to put forward false evidence to the court should the solicitor cease to act. In other circumstances, it would be for the court, and not the solicitor, to assess the truth or otherwise of the client's statement.

It is clear from these rules that the first obligation of an advocate before a legal court or tribunal is honesty and directness to the court. This obligation supersedes all others where it is in conflict with them. The court has to rely on the integrity of its advocates, especially within the adversarial system in which findings of fact are based entirely on the alternate or opposing views put by both advocates and in which the judge or tribunal may not, usually, become principally involved in the presentation of either side's case.

The need for such integrity is both paramount and absolute and the court (or tribunal etc.) will expect absolute honesty even in relation to the smallest detail such as reasons for adjournment, times of delivery of notices or letters etc. and even apologies for the advocate's own lateness of arrival.

Such an obligation is often in direct conflict with duties to the client and advocacy of one's case; but it is not usually in conflict with the duty to oneself and subsequent clients in the eye of the court or tribunal. It may therefore be helpful to propose the author's view of how the hierarchy of obligations beyond the duty to the court might be considered in turn by the advocate.

1.4.2   Duty to the profession

The penalty for not observing the professional rules of obligation to the court may be exacted by the court itself under the rules of contempt (and especially instant contempt) or may be referred to the appropriate professional body to enquire into the circumstances as a part of its disciplinary procedure. Although it will be permissible to advocate one's clients cause to the best of one's ability within the rules of court, it will never be permissible knowingly to mislead the court, especially with regard to the effect of a previous, reported or unreported case. In most instances the duty to the court and the professional obligations will coincide, but where there is a conflict between the professional duty and duty to oneself and duty to the client, the professional obligation should take precedence.

1.4.3 Duty to oneself

Although this may sound a very self-interested duty the obligations advocates have to themselves relate at least as much to their future clients as to their own well-being. Advocates must ensure that, wherever there is any doubt whatsoever, there own liability is safeguarded. This is not simply self-preservation but a means of ensuring that the advocate will be available for the next clients' cases and not fighting rearguard actions or effective appeals on previous clients' cases. Although the rule in *Rondel* v *Worsley* [1969] 1 AC 191 and *Saif Ali* v *Sydney Mitchell & Co.* [1980] AC 198 probably means that an advocate will not have liability in negligence for what has been done in advocating a client's case in a court or tribunal, such actions may arise out of initial advice, undertakings or questions of costs. Awards of costs against the lawyers involved in cases have become more frequent recently and all lawyers must guard carefully against this possibility. Similarly lawyers should guard against wasted costs through improper or unreasonable work or negligent acts or omissions. A book of this nature is not able to cover in detail how such issues may arise but books on the law of professional practice and recent cases should be considered where advocates are in any doubt of their position.

1.4.4 Duty to the client

According to the Bar's code:

5 Conduct of work

5.1   A barrister must at all times promote and protect fearlessly and by all proper and lawful means his lay client's best interests.

It may sound quite improper that the duty to the client should come so far down the list. In fact, if all the other obligations are kept to, it is likely that the obligations to the client will have been properly fulfilled. Although clients may not appreciate this at the time of trial, it is unlikely to be in their favour, in the long run, for a lawyer to mislead the court or for an untrue plaint or defence to be run. It is very easy to be caught out in a tangled web and a good advocate will certainly be trying as hard as possible to persuade the litigant to settle where a case is not as strong as it first appears.

1.4.5 Duty to the cause of justice

It is even stranger perhaps to see 'justice' as the very last obligation of the advocate. Hopefully, once again, before the preceding obligations have been set aside justice will have been done. But it does need to be addressed. An advocate is a 'mouthpiece' speaking on behalf of a particular client, but at some stage when the obligation to the client has been satisfied it may become necessary to do 'justice' more generally to others involved in a case or to some other socially desirable need.

'Justice' of course means very different things to different people. For each party it may mean that they win, but they cannot both have the same justice. For some it may mean 'mercy' and for others it may mean just retribution, even if that is a harsh penalty. The good advocate must see how best to fulfil the obligations of 'justice' in a particular case. When all else has been settled, it too needs attention.

1.5 SPECIAL ISSUES IN ADVOCACY

1.5.1 Formality

Other rules which are special to the legal advocate concern the formality of proceedings in each specific court or tribunal. By and large these concern forms of address, rules of turn-taking and rules concerning who can say what and when. Rules of address will be looked at subsequently and the other rules are considered here.

Advocacy is usually formal in courts and tribunals even though it may be possible for lay representation to occur in a particular forum. This is partly because respect has to be shown to the court and the person or persons carrying out the judicial function. It is also a means of controlling the language used within the setting, and probably a means of preventing non-lawyers from feeling at home in those settings. Colloquial terms and vernacular speech are usually avoided but advocates must be most careful not to pitch their representation above the level of a lay bench or jury. Nor should the advocate, unless for a particular purpose, make it difficult for a witness to understand the questions put.

1.5.2 Taking turns

Turn-taking exists even within a normal social conversation but is not so formalised as in a courtroom. As one person finishes speaking, over a coffee or a drink, the other person clearly realises that it is now his or her turn to say something. Usually an inflection at the end of a sentence, a direct look or simply the sense of the words spoken encourage the other party to be involved. This is rather more formalised in the courtroom, but its presence in familiar social settings means that it is not so difficult to adhere to.

The rules of procedure in each court or tribunal usually dictate who speaks first and last. In general these rules place the protagonist as first speaker and the person defending the claim or allegation as the last speaker. There are also particular rules about how many opening and closing speeches there are which are peculiar to each forum. By and large these allow each side to have a turn to put its own case and refute that of the other side. In planning advocacy it is essential to understand the particular procedure of the forum involved. This will dictate not only what to say and when, but will assist in a formulation of strategy.

1.5.3 What to say and when

In concert with turn-taking, only certain types of issue or speech may be addressed on each occasion or turn. For example, evidence should not be given by an advocate but by witnesses. An opening speech should merely set out a road-map of the evidence but not attempt to present it. Legal arguments should only be given in opening or closing addresses. Points made to a jury or other finder of fact should not be placed as an 'aside' to a question in examination or cross-examination. Advocates should know both what they intend to say and what they expect their witnesses to say. To some extent other 'turns' can be used to get over ideas which were missing from a previous 'turn' but the form of the approach has to be fitting to the form of that 'turn'.

For example, in the context of a hearing before a master in the High Court for summary judgment, an issue not mentioned in a preliminary statement on the part of the plaintiff may be introduced subsequently in answer to the defendant's responses. It would be necessary, though, to link the issue into the defendant's response. Similarly in the context of a full-scale hearing, an issue not raised in an opening speech might well be adverted to in the form of a question on examination-in-chief or cross-examination subsequently. In this case, it would be necessary to ensure the relevance of the question both to the witness and to the particular piece of examination or cross-examination.

In other words, although the system appears overly formal and organised, it is quite possible for the advocate to say what is required within a part of the procedure that is not obviously designated for such issues. All that is necessary is to find an appropriate way to introduce the issue.

1.5.4   You or your witness

An advocate must ensure that all evidence as such, in other words factual material or opinion related to the case, is developed by the witnesses in court rather than simply mentioned by the advocate. It is the advocate's duty to help the court to understand evidence which has been given and also to point out distinctions between the evidence given by both sides. It is also the duty of the advocate to point out and argue any questions of law arising from the evidence.

All of this must be contrasted with the evidence itself which must be heard directly out of the mouths of (or in the affidavit from) the witnesses concerned. If the evidence does not come from the witnesses it is not really before the court. Nothing said by an advocate, even one who knows what the witness might have intended to say, can change this fact. If a witness does not come up to proof the advocate must try very hard in examination of that witness to give the witness every opportunity to say what was expected. Failing that, the advocate must defend or argue the case on the basis of what the court has heard not what the advocate might have wished the court to hear.

1.6 SUMMARY

Advocacy is a subspecies of representation which in turn is a species of general oral communication. Many of the social rules involved in advocacy are more specific examples of rules learned in the more general context, but the special duties of the advocate are different.

The aim of this chapter has been to show that advocacy is not a completely new way of behaving which needs to be learned from scratch. The special duties of a legal advocate, and the particular legal rules within which such advocacy takes place, emphasise the particular difficulties of advocacy as a legal skill. Nonetheless, such a skill is founded, in part, on many of the social skills which, in less crucial contexts, we all take for granted. We are all involved every day in forms of oral communication and often in forms of representation. Behaving as an advocate is only a more specialised form of each of these. Neither is there any accepted mode or approach which has to be followed, like the television or film lawyer. Good advocates have local accents, an informal demeanour, and a pleasant approach as much as they might have plums in their mouths, distant expressions and an off-putting manner. It is therefore necessary to concentrate more on the objectives of the occasion than in aping the style of others.

Chapter Two

Preparation before the Day

As mentioned in the Introduction, advocacy itself is very much the tip of an iceberg. The greater bulk of the iceberg is below the surface unseen by the court and is carried out in terms of preparation prior to the hearing. This book will concentrate on later aspects of the preparation of a case as the hearing day approaches. Much of the work and skills involved in interviewing clients and witnesses, identifying appropriate issues, arguments and law will already have occurred. Many of the details of the case will already be defined by negotiation between opposing sides. Skills and work of this nature are considered by other books in this series and will therefore be largely assumed here. Such assumption is not to be made lightly. The character of the work in preparation for the hearing will be far more decisive of the ultimate outcome of the case than events on the day. This chapter will therefore be concerned more with preparation for the hearing itself than of the materials in the case.

2.1 PROCEDURE

To the lay person, the neophyte or inexperienced lawyer the practice and procedure within any particular court or tribunal appear to be based on esoteric knowledge only available to the initiated of some priesthood. Although it is clear that the atmosphere of each forum will be quite different (and both regional and judge-related variations abound) the basics of procedure in the

High Court, county court and tribunals and most other fora are well set out in rules and regulations of the court, tribunal or other forum. It is therefore first necessary to identify the source of such regulations and ensure a clear understanding of the expected procedure to be adopted on the occasion in question and before the forum in question.

The 'White Book' covering the High Court, the 'Green Book' covering the county court and the 'Blue Book' covering the magistrates' court are absolute bibles for the new advocate. Nothing should be done within those courts which is not allowed by the rule books in question. Tribunals are different and often depend on whether the chair of the tribunal is a lawyer or not. But for each tribunal a form of procedure is usually available either in the form of rules and regulations or advisory pamphlet material. In circumstances where no rules or regulations exist it is common for the chair or judge to set out procedures at the beginning of a hearing.

Proper preparation involves ensuring that the advocate is aware of the overall procedure at the hearing and any particular quirks which might be involved in the case in hand. Where certain procedural advantages might be possible for one side or other, these should also be carefully noted, so that they can be used or prevented if the occasion arises.

2.2 LAW

In early preparation of any case, especially one that is likely to go for hearing, there will have been a preliminary identification of the basic subject area of law and an investigation into the detail of the particularly relevant law in order to decide what factual investigation to undertake in preparation for trial.

Cases do change considerably from the early days of the first meeting with a client after which legal research will often take place. As further information, evidence and views arrive from the other side or other parties and witnesses, the nature of the factual information develops and therefore also the nature of the relevant law. Law itself also changes and it is quite possible that specific changes in law could occur between an early investigation and the time of a hearing or a full-blown trial. In any event it is necessary to clarify absolutely what is starkly relevant to the case in question, and what is not, within the days before the hearing.

It is hepful to identify in the form of a list what necessary ingredients must be proved, or could be proved, in order to substantiate the client's case. Although the statutes may be numerous, case law detailed and the textbooks verbose, each particular issue in a case will usually boil down to some three or four legal elements or ingredients. It is helpful to analyse these and set them out on paper with absolute clarity shortly before the day of the hearing. Such an analysis of ingredients in relation to a particular case might look like this:

Example: analysis of legal ingredients

You are acting for the Computer Employment Agency who claim to have introduced Jill Programmer to the defendants, Friendly Employers Ltd. In the pleadings Friendly have admitted that they initially received papers regarding Jill from the Agency, but rejected her at that time.

Subsequently, they allege that about a year later Jill was introduced to them by a mutual friend and then taken on by Friendly. By this stage, they claim, the original papers had been destroyed as the previous job had been filled.

The legal ingredients of your case might look like this:

   (a)   Contract between Agency and Friendly and terms of that contract.

   (b)   Performance by Agency of their part of the contract by introduction of Jill.

   (c)   Performance by Friendly of their part of the contract by hiring Jill.

(d)   The lapse of time, and any other intervening factors, between (b) and (c) above are not relevant.

The objective is to state as bluntly and as succinctly as possible what the law requires for your side to prove, or disprove, in the case to succeed. If necessary, the ingredients or issues can be broken down further into smaller elements on which to hinge particular facts. You will be developing a list of legal issues which need to be proved, or disproved, and will subsequently (see below) set out the facts which you will need to adduce in order to prove or disprove those issues alongside that list.

In some cases a defence, for example, might be shown in a number of ways. If sufficient facts are available for more than one approach, then each of those legal issues would need to be enumerated (although mentioned clearly as being in the alternative) so that the necessary facts can be set out against them.

The effect of this preparation is to have set out on one page the relevant law in brief and subsequently the relevant facts against that law. This will assist the advocate:

(a)   in preparing decisions on what evidence to lead and in which order;

(b)   in deciding what to say in an opening or closing speech; and

(c)   in making spur-of-the-moment decisions regarding the calling of further witnesses or adducing particular pieces of evidence or arguing certain questions of law.

It will therefore be a map of the case, and as the advocate passes through each point (which might not necessarily occur in a directly sequential fashion) that particular item can be ticked off as an element which has been proved.

Preparation of the relevant law in this manner may often need to be carried out right up until the very last days before a hearing because concessions regarding certain issues do occur at this point. Often additional factual material will have mounted up in the interim and will not necessariy have been taken fully into account. If the court is to understand with absolute clarity the case which the advocate is proposing, the advocate needs to have that case and its theme sufficiently clearly set out so that it can be transmitted onwards to the court. A great deal occurs through the ritual of the courtroom and the interaction of those involved in a court hearing. But the signal theme of your side's case should be heard clearly through all the other toing and froing which goes on. The theme should be uppermost in the mind of the advocate and all efforts throughout the other ritual should be aimed at stamping this theme into the minds of the court.

2.3 FACTS

In the same way it is necessary to prepare a clear vision of the relevant factual material shortly before the hearing. As explained immediately above, such factual material needs to be closely tied in to the necessary legal issues which must be proved or disproved.

It is therefore helpful to set out the facts in a skeleton list against the legal issues. In order to produce the available facts necessary to prove the law, the advocate will need to scan through all witness statements, proofs of evidence and any documentary evidence which will be available to the court. It is helpful then to list each item of evidence in the degree of its importance in proving a particular, necessary issue. Often an issue can be proved in more than one way. If one witness does not come up to proof on that item when examined in court then another witness might be available to prove that point. If the list sets out the names of the witnesses as well as the factual material in brief detail or headings then the advocate can use this map to navigate, in the fast-changing torrents of a trial, which particular path or waterway to take, which witnesses to call next and what areas to cover in most detail with them.

Example: skeleton map of law and facts

A mixed law and fact proof skeleton of the example case mentioned above could look something like this:

Item	*Law*	*Relevant facts and proof*
1	Contract between Agency and Friendly and terms of that contract.	Contract dated 20-9-91. Statement of Bill Comp. Evidence of Joe Friendly.
2	Performance by Agency of their part of the contract by introduction of Jill.	Letter dated 25-9-91. Statement of Bill Comp. Evidence of Joe Friendly.
3	Performance by Friendly of their part of the contract by hiring Jill.	Defence. Evidence of Jill Programmer. Evidence of Mr Friendly.
4	The lapse of time, and any other intervening factors, between 2 and 3 above are not relevant.	Arguments from Estate Agency. Cases on 'ready, willing and able purchasers'.

In organising your preparation of this road-map it is essential that you do not become too detailed in what you produce. Unless you are dealing with a trial or hearing lasting more than a day or two you should be able to boil all the issues down and all the facts to one side of a sheet of A4. If you have not done this then you may not be giving yourself a sufficiently stark overview of the case and the presentation of an overview to the court may become more complicated than necessary.

Having set out the skeleton or tree of facts and law necessary for proving the case, the advocate may well find it useful to prepare further each of the proofs of evidence or witness statements which are to be used in court. A useful suggestion is to reduce each page of witness statement on the photocopier so that a blank margin appears on one side or all around the statement itself. The elements within that page of the witness statement which are necessary to be proved can then be highlighted on the text and numbered in the blank margin. A page of witness statement, so treated, would then look like figure 2.1.

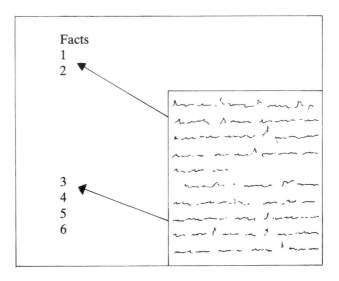

Figure 2.1   Analysed witness statement

This may seem a laborious method of preparation but it shows with absolute clarity the necessary items which each witness must prove in court. As will be seen later, when conducting an examination-in-chief, the advocate can then tick off each item as stated by the witness and listen clearly to what the witness is saying in order to ensure that the court has heard and understood all facts which need to be proved. If only the original statements by themselves are used during a hearing, the detail of the words expressed by the witness in the statements can make it difficult for the advocate to concentrate on whether the major issues have been addressed in the examination-in-chief.

In summary, then, there should be an overall map of both facts and law through which the whole needs of the trial can be addressed. There should also be detailed notes for each witness or other element of evidence to remind the advocate, especially in the heat of trial, what needs to be adduced in relation to that witness or material evidence.

2.3.1   Exchange of witness statements

Under new rules in the county court it is becoming mandatory for witness statements to be exchanged within set dates related to the close of pleadings. Preparing a witness statement for exchange with the other side adds a further dimension to the process. The drafted witness statement must itself look coherent, rational and strong — perhaps more so than if only for use by yourself.

Further, in some courts, it is now usual for the witness statement to stand in place of examination-in-chief. This will speed up the trial but will have other consequences. Witnesses will not have a chance to review their story in court before being cross-examined on it. The story will not be relayed by the witness before being attacked by the other side's advocate. Even under these new rules it will be helpful to prepare your case in the manner suggested above, to ensure that you know where all the facts you need to prove can be found.

2.4   WITNESSES

It is first of all necessary to consider the rules in the Guide to the Professional Conduct of Solicitors specifically applicable to witnesses:

14.05   Principle

It is permissible for a solicitor acting for any party to interview and take statements from any witness or prospective witness at any stage in the proceedings, whether or not that witness has been interviewed or called as a witness by another party.

Commentary

1   This principle stems from the fact that there is no property in a witness and applies both before and after the witness has given evidence at the hearing.

2   A solicitor must not, of course, tamper with the evidence of a witness or attempt to suborn the witness into changing his

evidence. Once a witness has given evidence, the case must be very unusual in which a solicitor acting for the other side needs to interview that witness without seeking to persuade him to change his evidence.

3   A solicitor should be aware that in seeking to exercise his right to interview a witness who has already been called by the other side or who to his knowledge is likely to be called by them, he may well be exposed to the suggestion that he has improperly tampered with the evidence. This may be so particularly where the witness subsequently changes his evidence. It is wise in these circumstances for such solicitor to offer to interview the witness in the presence of the other side.

4   In interviewing an expert witness or professional agent instructed by the other side there should be no attempt to induce the witness to disclose privileged information. In these circumstances also it would be wise to offer to interview the witness in the presence of the other solicitor's representative.

5   As a general rule, it is not improper for a solicitor to advise a witness from whom a statement is being sought that he need not make such a statement. The advice that the solicitor should give must depend upon his client's interest and the circumstances of the case.

6   A solicitor must not, without leave of the court, or without the consent of counsel or solicitor for the other party, discuss the case with a witness, whether his client or not, whilst the witness is in the course of giving evidence. This prohibition covers the whole of the relevant time including adjournments and weekends.

The Barristers' code states:

6.2   Save with the consent of the representative for the opposing side or of the court, a barrister should not communicate directly or indirectly with any witness, whether or not the witness is his lay client, once that witness has begun to give evidence until it has been concluded.

The Guide to the Professional Conduct of Solicitors continues:

14.06   Principle

A solicitor must not make or offer to make payments to a witness contingent upon the nature of the evidence given or upon the outcome of a case.

Commentary

1   There is no objection to the payment of reasonable expenses to witnesses and reasonable compensation for loss of time attending court. In the case of an expert witness, there is an implied obligation to pay a reasonable fee. (See also principle 10.21.)

2   A solicitor is professionally responsible for payment of the reasonable agreed fees and expenses of expert, professional and other witnesses whom he calls to give evidence on behalf of his client, unless a specific disclaimer is first conveyed to the witness. This obligation includes witnesses who have been subpoenaed where they have been invited to give evidence and have agreed to do so. Therefore, a solicitor who does not wish to accept such responsibility should make this clear to the witness in advance. In criminal cases in the Crown Court, all witnesses, other than expert witnesses, can obtain payment of their fees and expenses within the limits of the statutory scale, from the court office. It is good practice to inform such witnesses of this and to agree in advance whether the solicitor will accept responsibility for any sum in excess of such scale.

3   In legal aid cases, whether civil or criminal, a solicitor should draw the attention of the witnesses to the fact of legal aid and that the witnesses' fees and disbursements will have to be taxed or assessed and that only such amounts can be paid to the witness. A solicitor should expressly disclaim personal responsibility for payment of fees beyond those allowed on taxation or assessment. Practitioners are reminded that prior authority in respect of witnesses' fees and expenses can be obtained in civil and criminal cases from the area committee.

4 A solicitor, on his client's instructions, may insert advertisements for witnesses to come forward as to a particular occurrence. However, care must be taken to draft the advertisement so that, so far as practicable, it does not suggest the detailed testimony sought.

14.07 Principle

A solicitor must not accept instructions to act as an advocate for a client if it is clear that he or a member of his firm will be called as a witness on behalf of the client, unless the evidence is purely formal.

Commentary

1 A solicitor must exercise his judgment as to whether to cease acting where:

(a) he has already accepted instructions as an advocate and then becomes aware that he or a member of his firm will be called as a witness on behalf of the client; or

(b) he is instructed to act, but not as an advocate, and knows that he must give evidence.

2 The circumstances in which a solicitor should continue to act as an advocate, or at all, must be extremely rare where it is likely that he will be called to give evidence other than that which is purely formal.

3 It may be possible for a solicitor to continue to act as an advocate if a member of his firm will be called to give evidence as to events witnessed whilst advising or assisting a client, for example, at a police station or at an identification parade. In exercising his judgment the solicitor should consider the nature of evidence to be given, its importance to the case overall and the difficulties faced by the client of the solicitor were to cease to act. The decision should be taken in the interest of justice as a whole and not solely in the interests of the client.

Similarly the Bar conduct rules state:

501 A practising barrister must not accept any brief . . .

(d) if the matter is one in which he has reason to believe that he is likely to be a witness or in which whether by reason of any connection of his with the client or with the court or a member of it or otherwise it will be difficult for him to maintain professional independence or the administration of justice might be or appear to be prejudiced.

Beyond these rules of conduct, an English advocate is also not allowed to 'rehearse' a witness. This means that the advocate must not prepare the witness for testimony by taking the witness through an examination-in-chief or role-play cross-examination. The trial is supposed to be a special moment for testing the truth and its effect would be diminished by any rehearsal of such evidence. Interestingly, this is not the position in the United States. Indeed, President Abraham Lincoln had apparently perfected the art of rehearsing witnesses by walking them up and down the shed where the horses were kept outside the courtroom before a case: a practice which became known as 'horse-shedding'.

These rules are enshrined in the Bar's conduct provisions:

607.1 Save in exceptional circumstances and subject to paragraphs 607.2 and 609 a barrister in independent practice must not discuss a case in which he may expect to examine any witness:

(a) with or in the presence of potential witnesses other than the lay client, character witnesses or expert witnesses;

(b) with the lay client, character witnesses or expert witnesses in the absence of his professional client or his representative.

607.2 In a civil case a practising barrister may in the presence of his professional client or his representative discuss the case with a potential witness if he considers that the interests of his lay client so require and after he has been supplied with a proper proof of evidence of that potential witness prepared by the witness himself or by his professional client or by a third party.

607.3   A practising barrister must not when interviewing a witness out of court:

(a)   place a witness who is being interviewed under any pressure to provide other than a truthful account of his evidence;

(b)   rehearse, practise or coach a witness in relation to his evidence or the way in which he should give in.

If one cannot rehearse a witness, can the witness be prepared for what is going to occur in court? It is certainly possible for the advocate to help a witness to understand the procedure in court and to prepare for what is likely to occur when in the witness-box, without rehearsal. It appears that some firms of solicitors are preparing witnesses for the prospect of testimony by role playing 'testimony' on facts different from those involved in the case. This would appear to be within the rules since it does not help the witness to tell the story in a particular way but simply to be more used to the atmosphere in court.

There appears to be no difficulty in reminding a witness of his or her own witness statement by sending it to the witness a few weeks before the hearing in order to ensure that the witness is aware of what he or she said and signed and to see whether there is anything which the witness would like to reconsider. Even such a late reconsideration is more helpful to the advocate than learning on the day of the hearing, and even sometimes in full court, that a witness has decided to change a piece of testimony. The practice of ensuring a witness's continuing agreement to what he or she has said will also have the effect of jogging the witness's memory regarding events which may have occurred some time before the hearing itself. Where witness statements are exchanged with the other side, and this occurs a long time before the hearing itself, it may be necessary to seek amendment or adduce up-to-date testimony in court on new or changed issues.

The verbatim words taken down in a witness interview, in the exact form and order in which they occurred at the interview, need not be used when writing the proof of evidence to be used at trial. There is no difficulty in reproducing a more chronological, or ordered, statement provided that no new words or ideas are put into the mouth of the witness. Thus, even the most garbled version on first statement can be reproduced in a clear and ordered form. This will certainly also assist the subsequent relationship between the law and fact chart mentioned above and the witness statements. It will also be more appropriate for a witness statement that needs to be exchanged with the other side.

Witnesses need to be made aware of:

— when they are likely to be called to give evidence,
— that in criminal cases they will not be allowed to sit in court before they have given evidence,
— that they are likely to be cross-examined on the evidence (in some cases only cross-examined),
— and any other particular procedure of the court or forum.

Witnesses need to be warned as far in advance as possible of the date of the hearing and a *subpoena ad testificandum* prepared and served if necessary. Conduct money also needs to be tendered to a witness who might otherwise not be able to appear at the hearing and this should be tendered prior to the hearing in order to avoid any difficulty of that nature.

Witnesses' friends and clients' friends should also be made aware of the necessity to present themselves in an orderly way if they come to court. A good advocate might well warn a skinhead client or witness to come to court with forearm swastikas covered and also warn that the effect may be lost if a number of mates crowd the public gallery with theirs uncovered, chortling at every statement in the witness box.

Once the witness has arrived in court the courteous advocate will spend a little time with the witness, showing recognition, explaining where the witness must wait, attempting to assess when the witness is likely to be called and even pointing out available conveniences such as drinks machines and lavatories. Many advocates spend all their time in court talking to other lawyers involved in their case or other hearings. Prudent advocates look after their own witnesses because they are their artillery and weaponry. Witnesses must be kept willing and comfortable, as much as is possible in the circumstances. They will have worries and concerns and these should be addressed if the advocate wants each witness to perform in the manner desired.

Clients and other witnesses should also be told that it is sensible to turn a little towards the judge(s) when giving evidence. They should try to watch whether anyone is taking manuscript notes, such as the judge, or clerk in the magistrates' court, and if so should pause unitl that person has stopped writing.

The solicitor advocate has as much time as is necessary beforehand to write to the witness and should be prepared to spend time immediately prior to the hearing with the witness on the day itself (see also chapter 3).

2.5   OUTCOMES

It is all very well preparing law, procedure, facts and even witnesses. But it is also necessary to concentrate on the possible outcomes or remedial solutions of each case. In this context the advocate must prepare by checking both in law and procedure what possible decisions can be made by the court, tribunal or other forum; which of those decisions are desirable to the advocate's client; and how best to persuade the court to come to those particular decisions. Any trial preparation which does not also concentrate upon the most desirable and best alternative client outcomes might be perfect in itself but still not do justice for the client or the client's case.

Thus, even in a straightforward breach of contract case it is important to prepare whether the court can find or order (and whether the facts and law merit) rescission, damages, frustration, general and special damages, punitive damages etc., and what would be the most effective and most desirable of these solutions for your client.

Awareness of all the possible outcomes means awareness also of the possibility of losing and needing to mitigate any reasonably likely adverse decisions. The form of question which advocates should ask of themselves is:

What will I do if . . . (e.g., the court recognises the other side's breach but cannot see any damages flowing from it)?

In answering this question on each occasion the advocate should be prepared to try to find the best alternative for the client even in the face of the most adverse decision.

2.6 COSTS

Although the question of costs ought to be uppermost in the lawyer's mind it is surprising how often at best it is an afterthought in relation to negotiation and advocacy. A proper preparation of one's case means also considering what sort of costs orders to ask for from the court, where costs can be ordered, and what arguments should be put for any such orders to be made.

This must entail some knowledge of the usual orders in such cases as well as any procedurally different possibilities and any practical or strategic suggestions with regard to the other side's client being out of the jurisdiction or in financial difficulty etc.

In some particular cases, including acting as advocate for the prosecution, specific costs might be asked at the end of a hearing. These would need to be checked with the client and substantiated well before the hearing. In all other cases as well, costs need to be properly considered in preparing for a hearing and not simply left to the moment the decision is handed down by the court.

In preparing the case clients should be made aware of:

(a)   their own likely costs;

(b)   the risk of paying the other side's costs;

(c)   the effect of the statutory charge.

2.7 APPEALS

Another issue which is sometimes left unconsidered until too late is the question of what appeals might be available from this particular hearing. The question of appeals needs to be addressed from the point of view not only of losing but also of winning and defending the other side's attempt to appeal. In some cases the right to appeal can be granted by the court of first hearing, or of primary appeal. In such cases it is necessary to be ready to put arguments before the court on the basis of both law and procedure in order to defend or attack such right.

In other cases awareness of the possibility of appeal will require the immediate preparation of a 'case stated', for example, or full and proper advice to a client on receiving the result of the hearing. The existence and nature of the appeal needs to be researched as both a procedural and legal issue and time-limits need to be immediately noted and acted upon.

Careful preparation here will also assist in informing the client of the possibility of appeal. It is practice to do so in criminal cases and wise to do so in all cases.

With a range of outcomes, costs, orders and conditions of appeal in mind and prepared, the advocate will feel much more fully ready for fighting the hearing itself. The advocate will be secure in the knowledge of the best and worst results it might bring, and even more important, the advocate's own ability and confidence in dealing with whatever occurs.

2.8 YOUR DOCUMENTS AND COURT COPIES

The following elements of preparation before the day probably need to occur *after* the first seven mentioned above. Once the advocate is clear about those previous elements it will be sensible to begin to prepare the form in which the documents, if any, and court copies are to be placed together and presented. Often an agreed bundle of documents can be made up by both sides. This will of course need a prior degree of preparation so that any difficulties can be ironed out well before the documents go to court. It is always helpful to prepare an index and chronology and to paginate the contents.

Just like everything else in the preparation of one's case, the documents need to be set out with great clarity and in a manner and form intended to assist in proving the elements which have already been delineated above. Documents, then, are not simply a 'bundle' of necessary pieces of paper, but also part of the weaponry of the adversarial game and they need to be both organised and presented as such. Where possible, preference in contents pages and perhaps in order should be given to the items most necessary for proving the client's case.

Note carefully individual court and tribunal rules about how many copies of documents need to be given to the court and the other side, how many extras might be necessary for witnesses and always have an extra copy of important documents available.

2.9 THEIR DOCUMENTS

In some systems of procedure, documents which are to be presented to the court will be exchanged before preparation (and sometimes also an agreed bundle can be prepared, as mentioned above).

The advocate should also remember clearly any documents disclosed on discovery which are required to be produced in order to prove a piece of evidence or in order to challenge the other side's witness on cross-examination. The advocate must have a very clear idea, on the basis of the rules of evidence, of how those documents will be produced in court, in what circumstances they would be allowed as evidence, which witnesses should produce them and at what stage of their testimony. Documentary evidence is a detailed area of the law of evidence and if there is any doubt this should be consulted carefully. It cannot be assumed that all documents can at all times be presented to the court, tribunal or other forum. Particular tribunals will also have quite different sets of rules about evidence. sometimes the normal rules of evidence are quite relaxed and at other times they can be enforced more strictly than in a court of law.

2.10   AGREED ISSUES

By this stage of preparation you will be ready for the fray. Although there is still some measure of preparatory work relating to the actual conduct of the hearing which will be addressed in later chapters, at this point the advocate should be totally prepared on the issues involved in the case and also the applicable law, the likely outcomes and costs involved. This is therefore a good time to contact the other side in order to see whether the hearing can in any way be shortened or made less combative in relation to particular issues.

In the nature of legal work a full preparation of such details may not occur until shortly before the hearing. In any event the changes in both fact and law which can occur right up until the last minute often necessitate this form of approach. But, having taken a full account in the above way of all the issues, both sides may now be able to agree certain items. These include items or issues which would only cause more time and trouble in court to prove and may not actually be in contention or may not now be issues directly relevant to the case as it has finally developed.

Both sides may therefore wish at this stage to agree such issues and thereby save court time (an extremely valuable commodity) and possibly also reduce the number of witnesses to be called as well as the number of areas they would have to cover. This would also reduce the cost of the hearing for both parties as well as reducing the uncertainties of trial which at this stage may be highly desirable for advocates representing each party. It may also reduce the ire of a judge who does not wish to listen to hours of unnecessary evidence or argument.

The agreed issues can then be presented to the court as a part of the opening speech of the prosecution or plaintiff in the action.

Even if any discussions relating to the possible agreement of issues between the two sides fail, such discussions are very rarely wasted. The advocate will be aware of the feelings of the other side in preparation for the case and there may also be a heightened possibility of agreeing not only particular issues but also coming to a final negotiated agreement of the case itself. Whether or not any agreement results, the knowledge of the conversation will be useful in providing extra understanding of one of the unknown factors at trial — the tensions and the typical reactions of the other advocate.

2.11 AGREED LAW

Whilst attempting to agree issues or questions of fact, you should not forget to try to agree statements of law or of relevant cases before the hearing. An agreement of law may similarly reduce the number of facts which have to be proved, the number of witnesses to be called and also the necessary argument over law before the court or tribunal.

Law is often forgotten, and in any event does tend to become very much a backdrop to everything else occurring at trial. This is quite different when cases go on appeal. Appeals may be an even more fruitful occasion for agreeing issues of law and relevant cases prior to the hearing itself. The agreement could be in the form of a list of cases to be cited by both sides. Alternatively there could even be an agreed statement of both sides' understanding of the law.

2.12 CONFERENCE

The Bar rules suggest:

> 5.9   A barrister should be available on reasonable notice for a conference prior to the day of hearing of any case in which he is briefed; and if no such conference takes place then the barrister should be available for a conference on the day of hearing.

Solicitors should certainly proceed similarly.

2.13 CONCLUSION

Throughout this chapter I have referred to 'the other side' as if the hearing could only cover a two-party action. Many actions will be multi-party and this of course causes much more complexity than an action against a single, other party. However, the basics are still the same and as far as is possible any item concerning the other side should be taken up with each of the other parties.

In this chapter we have considered the range of items which need to be fully prepared before the day of the hearing. Preparation of the advocacy at the hearing itself will be looked at in chapters 4 to 8. But that advocacy will be made both possible and easier as a result of what we have already covered. Although not the stuff that television and film lawyers portray it is just as essential a part of the advocate's task as the hearing itself.

Chapter Three

On the Day

We have now reached the day of the hearing. All the patient work leading up to the hearing is about to reach its fruition. However, there is still a degree of mental and physical preparation which can only be carried out on the day itself and which will assist in easing the advocate's passage through the ordeal of the hearing.

3.1 DRESS

Certain courts expect even solicitors to be gowned. An advocate who is uncertain of the position should check with the court beforehand what is expected and what changing facilities exist. By and large, in Crown Court, open County Court hearings and in open High Court hearings gowns are expected. If so, clean and ironed wing collars should be prepared before the day and be available for the day. Studs and other elements of the collar all need to be ready and available so that there is no panic in the court changing rooms. Where gowns are not necessary, sober clothes should be worn and the advocate's appearance should always be well-groomed and sprucely clean. Apart from the resultant effect on natural self-confidence, it is a courtesy to the court to be dressed appropriately.

In recent times courts have made a number of comments on the dress of advocates appearing before them. If the judge says, 'I cannot hear you', it is more likely to be because you are not appropriately dressed than because the acoustics in the courtroom are poor or the judge is going deaf. On some occasions judges have complained about dirty fingernails and the absence of a waistcoat with a single breasted suit. Women solicitor advocates should follow the rules of dress for women barristers, when not gowned. This would include high-necked shirts and might also include long hair swept back and tied. Prominent jewellery is not advisable and can invite judicial comment. Details such as clean and shined black shoes are also important. Although such issues are of the utmost common sense they are of serious, extra importance in the courtroom setting. It is a major embarrassment to be told that you cannot be heard, especially if this occurs in front of the client.

According to the Guide to the Professional Conduct of Solicitors:

14.11   Principle

A solicitor appearing in court as an advocate should appear duly robed where this is customary and must always wear suitable clothing.

Commentary

1   Whilst it is proper for a solicitor or firm of solicitors to act as solicitors in a matter where he or the firm have an interest, they must, when engaged in such litigation, sue or appear as litigants in person. If they appear before the court in such a capacity, they should not be robed so that it is clear that they are not acting as professional advocates.

2   Where a solicitor, his employee or his firm is one of a number of plaintiffs or defendants, the firm is permitted to go on the record as the solicitors, but a solicitor or employee who is a party to the litigation should not appear as a professional advocate on behalf of the parties either in chambers or in open court. If he does appear he must not be robed; the alternative being for the litigants to be represented by some other person who can act as a professional advocate.

The Bar's code is similar:

5.12 In court a barrister's personal appearance should be decorous, and his dress, when robes are worn, should be compatible with them.

3.2   ADDRESS

Although before the day of the hearing it is possible to ascertain the likely level of judge who will be hearing the case, it is sometimes not certain until the day itself. There are also some major regional differences in the manner of address of different courts. It is therefore sensible to spend a little time with the court usher, court clerk, or other court official on the day of the hearing in order to ascertain the name, title and mode of address of the particular judge or judicial officer before whom you are appearing. This can be especially difficult where the judge is female as sometimes gender is to be recognised and sometimes not. There will also be some occasions on which the personal preference of the female judge needs to be ascertained in order to decide how she is to be addressed. A relaxed presentation will be assisted by ascertaining well beforehand how the judge or bench prefers to be addressed.

Broadly, a magistrates' bench should be addressed according to the gender of its Chair — either 'Sir' or 'Madam'. A County Court judge should be addressed as 'Your Honour' and a District Judge as 'Sir'. However, a new advocate should always check local or personal quirks.

An advocate addressing a panel should normally speak to the Chair of the panel but should also remember the other members during the hearing. Looking at them all whilst talking, at some points in the hearing is useful. It is not sensible, however, to look only at one wing member of a panel who appears to be sympathetic or receptive.

Demeanour is also important. Foppish or arrogant practices such as thumbs in waistcoat pockets, leaning back, smiling derisively while gazing at some distant corner of the ceiling should all be avoided — even if some members of the Bar use them.

3.3   PREPARING THE COURT

Exercise 1: the uninvited guest

This is the first of a series of exercises designed to be used in an introduction to advocacy course. They will be mentioned inside the body of the text because reading the exercises will be useful, even for those not taking part in them, as an introduction to what is involved in each stage of advocacy. Each will appear separated by a small ruled line in order to clarify its effect to the reader.

The complaint often heard from new advocates when they arrive for the first time at a new courtroom is that they feel somehow as if they are an uninvited guest at a party. Everyone else appears to know exactly where to go, who to talk to, which court they are in and what they should be doing. But, just like at a party where you have been brought by someone else who somehow gets detached from you as soon as you have been introduced to the host, there is a routine, or repertoire, of available strategies which can be used so that you too can find your way around the necessary people and places in this new court.

In this exercise each of the participants picks a piece of paper out of a hat. Each piece of paper has marked on it the name of a character in the court scene. For example if the court scene which is to be the subject of a role play is the magistrates' court, then the characters would typically be, e.g., prosecutor case 1, defending solicitor case 1, defendant case 1, defence witnesses 1-4, prosecution witnesses 1-5, court clerk, court usher, journalist, and even a set of magistrates.

This is an excellent warm-up exercise for beginning a course on advocacy. There is always some anticipation, delight and amusement as each person picks his or her character from the hat. They are not allowed to tell anyone else immediately who they are as this will develop as the exercise goes on.

Once everyone has selected a character and thought for a moment or two about what his or her character should do prior to the time of the hearing, the course leader explains that there is only a quarter of an hour before the appointed time of the hearing. Participants are reminded of how they are 'uninvited guests' at this 'party' and that they must use the same types of skills as they would at a party to find out who is who outside this courtroom and to make contact with the people with whom they need to do some business before the hearing starts.

Thus, for example, each advocate must identify and contact all of the witnesses for his or her side, make them at home and ensure their comfort and understanding of what is to occur.

A special case in this context is that of expert witnesses. Even in a criminal case they are allowed to stay inside the court during the entire hearing of the case so that they can comment on any other evidence which has been heard in the case. However, special permission needs to be obtained in order to organise that the expert witness be allowed to be present. On some occasions this can be negotiated prior to the hearing itself from the clerk of the court and on other occasions it may be necessary to ask permission from the judge at the beginning of a hearing. Even if the court clerk cannot organise or agree the issue, it is helpful raising it right at the beginning because this information might well be passed up to the bench in order to prepare them for the decision.

Each advocate needs to make contact with the court usher, give the court usher the advocate's name and obtain as much information as possible from the court usher about the judge, form of address and seating inside the courtroom. The latter is especially important since courts can have very different seating arrangements for barristers, solicitors or other representatives. Also, if there are a number of cases to be heard, fixed at the same time or throughout the day, there are often customary ways for people to sit in order to ensure that the advocates are in place when their turn comes for their hearing. In some courts this goes according to the order of the case list and in others according to the seniority of the advocates.

The usher will give the names of the advocates through the clerk, or directly to the judge. Therefore pronunciation of difficult names should also be explained to the usher so that there is no embarrassment within the courtroom.

In our 'uninvited guest' game as in the real courtroom the advocates also will need to contact the clerk, inform the clerk how many witnesses are likely to be called and warn the clerk of any cases which are to be referred to during the hearing. This will allow the clerk to prepare the availability of such cases for the judge or judges if the advocate wishes to refer to them directly.

Your client

Another one of the little pieces of paper to be drawn out of the hat is that of the defendant (if we are in a criminal court). The defendant may well be your client as defence solicitor or barrister. In the criminal court the defendant, or client, will certainly be in the court the whole time. In civil courts as well the client will be present throughout the hearing or trial.

It is vital to remember that helping your client is the objective of the enterprise rather than showing how friendly you are with all the other lawyers in the court. If the client is unaware of this type of proceeding it should be explained carefully and patiently to the client so that the client understands what is going to happen, what is happening at the time and afterwards what has happened.

Lastly, both in our game and in real life, it is sensible for the advocate to make contact with the advocate on the other side to agree any last-minute issues of fact or law. It is also useful to check whether the advocate is the same person with whom you have been negotiating throughout the preparation of the case in order to gauge the level of the advocate's knowledge of facts or whether it is somebody who has come in at the last moment, such as a barrister, to undertake the necessary advocacy.

Apart from individual issues of fact and law which can be agreed right up until the last minute, provided the advocate is fully prepared to do so, it will often be possible to agree a settlement of the entire action even at this late stage. Many cases do settle at this point in time and it is always worth trying to settle right up until the last moment.

In the quarter of an hour allowed for the exercise to progress, people introduce themselves to each other and thereby slowly make their way around those with whom they need to talk. Someone tells the journalists where they can sit and the journalists probably try quite hard to find out as much information as possible about the cases whilst advocates etc. may feel it is best not to talk to the press. Clerk and usher wait calmly for others to approach them. Witnesses look lost and then are told where they must wait and finally by the end of the 15 minutes everyone is just about sorted when the course leader calls on the first case.

After the exercise, it is sensible to debrief the players asking them what they did and who they talked to and what they managed to achieve in preparing the court before the hearing. Through the debriefing the trainer can point out all the issues as mentioned above which need to be dealt with and confirm that all players have a full understanding of what the advocate should be doing prior to the hearing.

3.4 CONCLUSION

Good advocacy needs a great deal of preparation before the day of the hearing in order to succeed. Such preparation would include summarising the law, facts and procedure relevant to your case, involving your witnesses and ensuring your own full understanding of all likely outcomes, appeals and costs ensuing. But, on the day it also needs attention to physical preparation of oneself as advocate. Make absolutely sure that you leave yourself enough time to find the courthouse on the morning of the hearing and that there is at least a good half hour before the hearing in order to allow you time to change, time to talk to all the people with whom you must connect and ensure the proper preparation of all things necessary to occur before the hearing.

Always get to court early. Those living in large towns can so often find themselves caught up in traffic or station closures or anything else that interrupts a journey. It is taken to be rudeness to the court if an advocate is late for a hearing and this cannot do either you or your client any good. Also, keeping calm and well-prepared needs attention to such common-sense details especially for less practised advocates.

We are now ready for the hearing itself.

Chapter Four

Pre-trial and Preliminary Hearings

This chapter considers what in general needs to be known in order to deal with pre-trial hearings or preliminary hearings but not for full actions or trial. A number of purposes lie behind such preliminary hearings. They are usually intended:

(a)   as a means of organising or shortening the trial itself;
(b)   to bring the parties together in the hope that the case might settle; or
(c)   as disposition hearings on questions of bail etc. when the evidence and the advocates are still preparing themselves for trial.

Such preliminary hearings can also be a mixture of two or more of these different elements.

In order to prepare for such a hearing it is necessary to ensure the advocate has complete knowledge of the purpose of the hearing and of the possible results which can occur. It is possible, for example, for final decisions to be made at some pre-trial hearings if both or one of the parties does not appear.

4.1   OUTSIDE THE DOOR OF THE COURT

Remembering the second of the purposes mentioned above for having pre-trial reviews every possible opportunity should be taken to take a case a little bit further along the road to negotiated settlement. Early meetings between the parties and their representatives at pre-trial or preliminary hearings are good occasions for this and, however stoney-faced the opposition, there is always some opportunity to take the contested issues a little bit further. Sometimes the other side is ready for this just before going into court and at other times (see later) it is better to push for settlement after the hearing.

Solicitors should also be mindful of rule 14.04:

14.04   Principle

Except when making an application to the court, a solicitor must not discuss the merits of the case with a judge, magistrate or other adjudicator before whom a case is pending or may be heard, unless invited to do so in the presence of the solicitor or counsel for the other side or party.

Commentary

1   If a written communication is to be made to the judge, magistrate or other adjudicator at any time, the solicitor should at the same time deliver a copy of it to his professional adversary or to the opposing party if he is not legally represented. Where oral communication is proper, prior notice to the other party or his solicitor or counsel should be given.

2   Where, after a hearing, judgment is reserved and a relevant point of law is subsequently discovered, a solicitor who intends to bring it to the judge's attention should inform the advocate on the other side, who should not oppose this course of action, though he knows that the point of law is against him.

4.2   MAKING THE RUNNING

Whether or not the pre-trial hearing has a specific objective or whether it is a fairly perfunctory exercise which needs to be gone through in order to move on to the next stage or procedure, it is important that at the hearing it is very clear to the other side and to the judge, master etc. that it is you and your side who are making the running.

This means that you have to identify a direct, particular strategy in relation to the objectives of the particular hearing which either gives you whatever advantage is possible in the particular context or ensures the minimum of disadvantage. Often such an advantage can be achieved simply by being the advocate who most adequately represents the issues in the case. In most hearings there will be a given order for who should open (and give the first speech). Normally it is this person who describes briefly what the case is about and the objectives of the particular hearing. However, it is always possible for the other side to reinterpret the case and the objectives during the course of the hearing so that their view is also properly reflected in any decision made subsequently.

Where issues have been agreed ouside the door of the court then 'making the running' includes informing the judge, District Judge, Master etc. of those agreements during the opening speech.

4.3   SUCCINCT BUT READY

Judges etc. will probably be listening to a number, sometimes a large number, of similar preliminary hearings in one session. They do not want each hearing to be long and drawn out. The objective of the advocate is therefore to be as succinct as possible in deciding what to say. However, proper preparation means that if it does become necessary to address the issues in more detail, the advocate is always ready to do so, but takes instructions and non-verbal direction from the judge. This involves a certain amount of flexibility of approach. Thus it is not such a good idea to learn off by heart what you want to say, but rather to understand the issues and be ready to deal with them at an appropriate length according to the demeanour and patience of the judge and degree of fight put up by the other side.

4.4   ANTICIPATING THE POTHOLES

Just as when driving along an unknown road the driver should be aware of the possibility of a sudden appearance of a pothole, the advocate at a preliminary hearing should always be aware of the possibility that what appears to be a perfectly straightforward hearing and procedure may well turn out to have a number of bumps or potholes in it. Some swerving or other anticipatory action may be necessary in order to avoid the obstacles either present or put in the way of the advocate by the other side or the judge.

This is a similar point to being 'succinct but ready'. The good advocate has the flexibility to handle each item as a straightforward norm, or else as a major fight which needs to be argued from absolute basics onwards including quoting chapter and verse of appropriate cases. A good, passing knowledge of the White Book, Green Book and Blue Book will enable the advocate to be ready for whatever comes. The awareness that there may be potholes down the way and that swerves should not be so great as to land the vehicle of advocacy off the road, will also be helpful.

4.5   THE PRE-TRIAL REVIEW

A pre-trial review is now an essential part of most default and non-default summons procedures in the county court. Appearances are invariably before a district judge and among the other decisions to be made are whether the case should go through to the small claims procedure or not. All claims below £5,000 will now automatically go through to the small claims procedure unless the district judge accepts that there is something special or difficult about the case, and there is some objection by one party or another to the case being tried under the small claims procedure. Other issues to be decided include many of those which will be discussed in 4.6.

Even a case worth more than £5,000 can be tried under the small claims procedure if both parties agree. Such issues should therefore be considered carefully before entering the district judge's room.

On a pre-trial review in the county court it is possible to obtain judgment against a defendant who does not appear. The advocate for the plaintiff should be fully aware of such possibilities and how to go about requesting them should the defendant not appear.

4.6 THE ORDER FOR DIRECTIONS

In the High Court the most similar alternative is a summons for directions which can be issued in the Queen's Bench Division. The normal form of the possible orders that may be made is as follows:

Order for Directions

1 This action be consolidated with other action(s).

2 The action be transferred to an official referee, and that the costs of this application be costs in the cause.

3 The action be transferred to Exminster County Court under section 40 of the County Courts Act 1984, and that the costs of the action, including this application be in the discretion of the County Court.

4 The plaintiff have leave to amend the writ as shown in the document initialled by the master and that service of the writ and the defendant's acknowledgement of service do stand and that the costs incurred and thrown away by the amendment be the defendant's in any event.

5 [The plaintiff have leave to amend the statement of claim] or [The defendant have leave to amend the defence (and counterclaim)] [The plaintiff have leave to amend the reply (and defence to counterclaim)] or as shown in the document initialled by the master, and to reserve the amended pleading within 28 days and that the opposite party have leave to serve an amended consequential pleading, if so advised within 14 days thereafter and that the costs of and occasioned and thrown away by the amendments be the defendant's [the plaintiff's] in any event.

6 [The plaintiff serve on the defendant] or [The defendant serve on the plaintiff] within 14 days the further and better

particulars of his pleading specified in the document initialled by the Master.

7 The plaintiff within 14 days serve on the defendant and the defendant within 14 days serve on the plaintiff a list of documents (and file an affidavit verifying such list) [limited to the documents relating to the special damages claimed] [or as may be].

8 There be an inspection of the documents within   days of the service of the lists (and filing of the affidavits).

9 The [defendant] retain and preserve pending the trial of the action the subject-matter of the action [or describe the property in question].

10 [Set out fully and precisely any other directions intended to be applied for (e.g., adducing expert evidence, etc.). [For example,] photographs of the subject-matter of the action be agreed if possible, for use at the trial of the action.

11 Both parties having agreed as to adducing expert evidence and as to the disclosure of experts' reports, they have leave to call expert evidence limited to one witness for each party.

12 Trial. Place: London. Mode: judge alone
Listing category: warned
Estimated length: five days. To be set down within 28 days.

13 The costs of this application be costs in the cause.

Often there will be questions about when discovery should occur and any special considerations about discovery will be dealt with on this occasion. The number of witnesses and number of expert witnesses may well also be covered at this hearing. These are essential issues for the proper running of a civil trial and need to be considered very carefully even at this early stage in preparation for the main trial. Limiting numbers of witnesses should be fought against quite hard if you feel that it is against your client's interests. Full arguments should therefore be considered on all of these issues beforehand and at least a mental eye if not a careful pencil should scan through each of the possible items on the summons for directions to enquire which of these items either you or the other party might want.

Some other important issues relate to requests for an undertaking for costs where the plaintiff is out of the jurisdiction. Similarly there are issues relating to service and discovery where the defendant is out of the jurisdiction or questions of costs where the defendant is given leave to defend but is out of the jurisdiction.

4.7 SUMMARY JUDGMENT

A form of hearing which is not really a preliminary hearing but is of a pre-trial nature, is the hearing on a summons for summary judgment under Order XIV of the Rules of the Supreme Court 1965 in relation to Queen's Bench Division work and similar forms of summonses which exist elsewhere. The result of such a hearing can be a judgment and although there is appeal under certain circumstances from this judgment the hearing will effectively be the trial. However, it is often used tactically or strategically as a means of putting pressure on the defence even where the plaintiff does not think that there is a very good chance of obtaining summary judgment. It can also be used to force disclosure of the details of defence evidence or force an interim payment.

The summons can be issued in all circumstances where no real defence has been served. This means that even if a paper defence has been served, but it does not disclose a real defence known to law, summary judgment can still be applied for and granted.

The general rules set out above, ensuring that you are aware of what can be requested and when, apply especially here. Issues of fact and evidence will be taken for granted where they are pleaded but the question of law of whether they disclose a legal defence is what will be considered in this form of hearing. This means that strong preparation on the legal issues is necessary and, even if you are clear that the facts suggested by the other side are completely untrue, you have to deal with these on a completely objective basis and can only deny them with opposing facts of your own stated without emotion.

Where the defence puts up a sufficient smokescreen with regard to questions of fact the judge may feel that a full trial is the only way in which such issues could be properly considered.

An Order XIV is an excellent way to start on advocacy. It does not involve witnesses: they are not conducted in open court; and the issues are often discreet and straightforward. However, it does involve arguing questions of law and such argument is often more the province of an appeal court hearing than the trial itself, where questions of fact usually predominate. This is why barristers are often asked to appear on summary judgment applications. The other reason is that their importance can be enormous. If it is possible to obtain an immediate judgment and not to have to wait a long time and for a full-blown trial with many witnesses and enormous costs the application for summary judgment can be crucial.

4.8   NOTING THE DECISION

At the end of a hearing the district judge, master or other judge will give the decision which may be phrased formally or informally as an order or judgment of the court. There is often not very much warning that this is going to occur and the judge may begin fairly suddenly indicating that he or she does not wish to hear any further representations and is ready to give the decision. This indicates the end of the hearing as far as the representations are concerned and it is not usually sensible to try to say anything further at this stage.

You should have your pen and notebook ready to note down the exact details of the decision or order which is made. If it is your summons, you may well have to draw up the order itself and will therefore need to have a very good idea of what was decided, although there may well be a particular form in which the order should be drawn up. Even if it is not your summons or application, it is a very good idea to ensure that you have a note of the decision made so that you can check on the details of the order subsequently drawn up by the other side. Indeed, if there is any disagreement about what was actually decided such notes will prove useful and may need to go before the district judge or master in order to help the judge's memory about what was actually decided.

It is a good idea to take down every word stated although this may be difficult in the circumstances. Therefore some forms of shorthand are often developed by counsel with, e.g., 'O' standing for order, 'P' standing for plaintiff, 'D' standing for defendant etc.

4.9 THE QUESTION OF COSTS

It may not be possible to address the question of costs until such time as the judge has conveyed to you the decision or order regarding the hearing. Once the decision has been given you need to be completely ready to deal with the question of costs. Normally, costs will follow the event which means that whoever wins gains the party and party costs of that hearing from the other side. However, many preliminary hearings are organised to forward the main proceedings of the case and nobody is the winner. This means that costs can be in suit/cause/application/or reserved or that each side would have to bear its own costs. Where, however, there is any possibility of asking for costs against the other side you should consider doing so. If the order for costs you are requesting is not the usual order it is sensible to make a reasonable argument for such an unusual order, such as the fact that the hearing was unnecessary and was simply a tactical measure by the other side, or that an offer had been made in relation to the hearing and prior to it, which offer was similar to the order made by the judge at the hearing. Demeanour is important on such occasions. Judges are not impressed by somebody gloating over a win or trying to rub salt into the wound of the other side's defeat. However, a reasonable request for costs where the other side were clearly acting irresponsibly or unfairly or unreasonably will usually be heard and sometimes granted.

Where you are acting as advocate for the loser of such a hearing you should be ready to defend any such question of costs in a similar, reasonable fashion. Costs are always a difficult question to handle because the hearing appears to be over and everyone has begun to turn off all of their energy. Suddenly everything has to be turned on

again in order to argue what is, after all, usually a crucual issue for
the clients as well as the lawyers.

This book does not list or discuss the relative merits of different
costs orders or systems for taxation, but the advocate should be
aware of these in preparation for the hearing.

4.10   ALWAYS OBLIGED

Whatever the result, whether you consider it to be good, bad or
indifferent; whether you have won or lost, you must always express
your thanks for the decision in the appropriate way. Usually this
means stating that you are 'obliged' as in, 'I am obliged, Master'.
Although such formalities seem a little unctuous at first, they
become part of your repertoire very quickly and it means that you
are considered as being a part of 'the club' and not different from
everyone else. All of this is part of 'playing the game' and you
should be prepared to do it just as much as everyone else, at least
when you start your experience as an advocate. After further
experience you can select an appropriate style and demeanour
which you feel works for you.

Solicitors should also be aware of rule 14.09:

14.09   Principle

A solicitor must comply with any order of the court which the
court can properly make requiring him or his firm to take or
refrain from taking some particular course of action; equally, a
solicitor is bound to honour his undertakings given to any court
or tribunal.

Commentary

1   A breach of this principle may amount to contempt of court.
(See also principle 17.15.)

2   A solicitor must not aid and abet his client where the client
refuses to obey a lawful court order.

3   The Society has issued guidance as to the steps a solicitor should take to secure the attendance of his client at the Crown Court for trial. (See Appendix C22 of the Solicitors' Code of Conduct.)

4.11   OUTSIDE THE DOOR OF THE COURT

The hearing is over and you are outside the door of the court either delighted with your success or rather less pleased with not having quite got what you had wanted or expected. But you managed. You succeeded in working your way through your first essay in advocacy.

Now is the time when you may want to run away to celebrate or to hide, but there are still two important tasks to be carried out before you leave the court.

It may well be that you have to go to a court office immediately to have an order drawn up by the court or to effect some further procedure started by your hearing.

But you should also remember the other side. Whether you have won or lost, having gone through the hearing together will often make it easier for an agreement to be reached at this stage. Sometimes, even if they have succeeded at this hearing, they will feel more apprehensive about succeeding at the trial itself. This is therefore another excellent opportunity to initiate the possibility of negotiation. Quite often the clients or one client are there and this also makes it a good opportunity to press for settlement or even have a settlement agreed. Another book in this series specifically discusses the question of negotiation and should be considered in relation to negotiation outside the door of the court.

4.12   KEEPING THE CLIENT WITH YOU

The advocate, in appropriate circumstances, should have in mind the solicitors' conduct code, 14.08:

14.08   Principle

Where a client, prior to or in the course of any proceedings, admits to his solicitor that he has committed perjury or misled the court in any material matter in continuing proceedings in relation to those proceedings, it is the duty of his solicitor to decline to act further in the proceedings, unless the client agrees fully to disclose his conduct to the court.

Good practice also suggests that whether your client has been with you at court or not you should immediately report to the client what happened at the hearing and what effect this will have on the conduct of the rest of the case. It is often especially difficult to consider doing this when you are personally either flushed with the success of the moment or disappointed with the result. It is important to remember that the entire objective of the proceedings is not the ego of the advocate but the needs of the client. You will find yourself drawn in to spending more time with the solicitors and/ or barristers on the other side than your own client, if you are not careful. This is a very bad lawyer's reaction. The client is all-important, will be much more uncertain of the court proceedings than you and find it all very much more strange and bewildering. The client needs to be kept with you in understanding what is going on and supporting the view and approach that you take all the way along. If therefore the client has been with you at the beginning of the hearing and throughout this hearing you should have spent some time explaining what was likely to occur.

Even if you have had the client with you and have spent some time explaining orally what has happened at the meeting, you must report to the client fully in writing subsequently. This is of course even more important when the client was not present at the hearing.

In dealing with the press, solicitor advocates should also remember rule 14.12:

14.12   Principle

A solicitor who on his client's instructions gives a statement to the press must ensure that he does not become in contempt of court by publishing any statement which is calculated to interfere with a fair trial of a case which has not been concluded.

4.13 CONCLUSION

In this chapter we have looked at pre-trial and preliminary hearings as a separate form of advocacy. Many new advocates begin to pick up their skills at such hearings. In some ways they are characteristic of full trials and in some ways not. Often they can be just as important as the full trial. Sometimes they can also be more difficult. In a trial there will be a number of occasions when particular views can be expressed in different ways. In a short hearing, when a judge etc. has a long list of similar hearings, it can be much more difficult to get one's point across in a precise and concise fashion. Preparation for such hearings must take this factor into account.

Chapter Five

Trial: Opening and Examination-in-chief

At last we have reached the trial itself. Getting to this point has been quite a feat of work and the reader may have tired of all the necessary preparations. Nothing though is quite so glorious for the newer advocate as to face a court totally prepared and ready for whatever surprises the trial may bring.

The parts of a major hearing or trial may be divided into:

(a)   Preparing the court (see 3.3).

(b)   Opening speech (see 5.1).

(c)   Examination-in-chief (see 5.2).

(d)   Submission of no case to answer (see 5.3).

(e)   Cross-examination (see 6.1).

(f)   Reexamination (see 6.2).

(g)   Closing speech (see 6.3).

(h)   Plea in mitigation (see chapter 7).

(i)   Mopping-up operations (see chapter 8).

Although different hearings will have slightly differently organised turns (and, for example, not everyone will have an opening speech nor will everyone have a closing speech), this is a sensible basis for handling all the skills which are necessary at most trials and hearings.

Preparing the court has been dealt with in chapter 3 on preliminary hearings. It is of equal importance for a full trial and chapter 3 should also be read in preparation for a trial.

5.1   THE OPENING SPEECH

Remembering the preparation which will have occurred right up until a few moments before the trial begins, the advocate should be ready with the particular address necessary for the judge concerned, knowledge of the name of the opposing advocate and an awareness of the basic procedure to be applied at the trial. It will usually be the prosecution or the plaintiff who will give the opening speech.

We will look at the skills involved in presenting the opening speech through the medium of our next three exercises: the road-map; the do-it-yourself person; and the visit of the Martian. As before, the exercises will be useful for a training course but will also be sufficiently descriptive for any reader to understand what is involved. The conclusion will then identify the necessary content of the opening speech.

Exercise 2: the road-map

The participants are divided into pairs. In each pair one person is designated as 'the driver' and the other person is designated as 'the guide'.

The objective is for the guide to describe how to go by car from point A to point B. Points A and B should be well-known to both parties who should also know pretty well the road between them. The guide has to describe within one minute how to get from A to B, noting all the major landmarks without giving any more information than necessary and thereby running out of time.

In order to keep up the feeling of competition the driver should be the one who selects what points A and B are and judges how well the guide has performed. At the end of the first exercise the two participants swap over roles and see whether the second attempt is better than the first as they negotiate a different route for a different pair of points A and B.

The objective here is to show how best to describe something which someone else is to go through whilst only giving them a limited number of signposts and places to find on the way. Too much information will be boring and will take too long. Too little information will not be adequate for the task of getting the driver to point B.

In the same way an opening speech must concentrate very carefully on just giving enough information. If there is too much then the judge or judges may become disinterested and not take in what they are being told. If there is too little information they will not be able to follow the evidence when it is finally given.

Exercise 3: the do-it-yourself person

This exercise makes a very similar point. For the purposes of this exercise the party atmosphere which was begun in exercise 1, preparing the court, is continued for a while. The participants are divided up into threes. In each trio there is a 'DIY person', an 'expert' and a 'kibitzer'. At the party the DIY person has found out that there is an expert in the particular area of home improvements which the DIY person needs to know about. It could be a question of plumbing, woodwork, masonry, electrics or anything else.

The expert, whose job it is to carry out work of that nature does not really wish to be disturbed on questions like this at parties. So the DIY person has to devise a strategy saying just enough about the difficulty in order to interest the expert and not too much so that the expert simply says, 'Why don't you come to my shop in the morning'. The kibitzer is just a third person who is not involved in either the interests of the DIY person or the expert and tends to interrupt and even change the subject on occasion. 'Kibitzer' is a Yiddish word for someone who gives unwelcome advice to others at a card game, drives from the back seat of the car, etc.

The objectives for this exercise will probably be clear from the exercise above. The introduction of a kibitzer here represents a fictional adversary who might just complain if an advocate says more than should be said in the course of an opening speech.

Exercise 4: the Martian comes to Earth

In this exercise the contents of the opening speech are considered. When you have worked with a case for a long time, right from the moment that your client walked through the door of your office, through the preparation of witness statements and legal research etc., you will know a great deal about it. In fact, you may not be able to see sufficiently the wood for the trees. Imagine then that you find yourself in front of someone who has absolutely no idea what your case is about. The judge is in this position. You therefore have to begin with absolute basics in explaining to the judge or judges what this case is about. The judge might as well be a visitor from Mars.

In the exercise one of the participants in the course is selected or asked to volunteer. That person is told that he or she is in audio but not in video contact with a visitor from Mars. In other words the visitor from Mars — who should be the trainer — can hear but not see the course participant.

The course participant is then asked to describe something fairly common, but a little complex, such as 'how to tie your tie', to the Martian. Another topic could be 'starting your car' or 'tying your shoelaces' or something of the sort. Nearly always the course participant takes for granted that the Martian understands about human limbs — arms, fingers and the position of each limb with regard to each other. Only halfway through does the participant realise that the human body needs to be explained so that the Martian can understand what is being described.

In the same way it is necessary to think of all judges as Martians in relation to a particular case until you have described the basis of the case or they show in some way a good level of understanding.

On debriefing the group after this exercise, which can be played through consecutively with different people, the trainer should consider with them whether in some cases it might be necessary even for an opening speech to include photographs or plans or maps or drawings or even a video, or scale models, to show to a judge. It is clear that such items would need to be agreed with the other side prior to the trial, but they may well be very helpful in bringing a judge up to a greater level of understanding than a Martian within a very short period of time. They will often be helpful for both parties to use during the course of the trial. Visual aids are useful for almost every form of presentation and should not be ignored for advocacy where their use can be helpful either to the understanding of the judges or jury or to the speed of the trial.

5.1.1   Content of the opening speech

In summary, therefore, the opening speech has got to be as succinct as a road-map. Succinct enough to be a good road-map in order to show the judges where to go but not too detailed so that it loses them. The opening speech should be enough to interest an expert but not so much that they get turned off. Lastly it should start from the very basics of the case remembering how much you had to learn as the lawyer involved right from the beginning.

The opening speech should summarise the issues. This will not be difficult for you since your skeleton plan of law and fact will set out exactly what you need to show and what you need to prove for the case to be decided in your interest. All that is necessary now in the opening speech is to summarise exactly what is stated on your one page of A4 in brief. The only slight difference here is that it will be necessary also to explain not just your side of a case but what the issues are from the point of view of both sides (explained of course from your point of view).

The skeleton map of law and facts considered in chapter 2 will be the basis for your opening speech since it summarises the necessary law and the ingredients of the case. The above exercises help to explain the manner in which that plan should be presented. It will be helpful to look again briefly at those sections in order to remember what that skeleton plan might include, and to visualise how you might present it.

5.2 EXAMINATION-IN-CHIEF

Leading your witnesses through their testimony is the most important part of presenting your case, since only testimony counts as a presentation of the facts upon which your arguments are based. The newer procedures in which witness statements will stand as evidence-in-chief will undermine the orality of proceedings and change the nature of the trial. Advocates should be prepared (and prepare their witnesses) for both approaches until procedure becomes more settled.

A practising barrister:

610(d)   must not adduce evidence obtained otherwise than from or through his professional client or devise facts which will assist in advancing his lay client's case.

We will first look at what is involved in examination-in-chief through the medium of the following exercises:

(a)   Understanding blocks.

(b)   The contours of the carpet.

(c)   The gestatory period of the African elephant.

(d)   *Vive la différence.*

Exercise 5: understanding blocks

For this exercise it is best to have some sets of children's building blocks. The wooden ones are best, but any will do. The blocks should be divided up into exactly equal pairs of sets of about five blocks in each. For example, a good set might include a flat oblong yellow, a blue rectangular thick block, a yellow triangle, a blue cube and a green arch, provided you have an extra of each item. You must ensure that you can put together an exactly equal set of blocks for two players.

The group is divided into threes, each trio containing participants who will then nominate themselves as A, B or C. C is told that C's job will always include keeping the time and so C must have access to a watch with seconds on it. This exercise goes through three iterations.

Iteration 1

A and B are each given a set of blocks for which the other person has the exactly equal other set in the pair. Then, facing each other, A is asked to bulid some sort of construction with the blocks in A's set. When A is finished A must signify to C that B can begin to copy this construction. C watches B make the copy and notes down how long it takes for the copy to be made, how accurate the copy is and what sort of mistakes occur.

At the end of this iteration the trainer explains that life would be very easy in the court of law if all that was necessary was for the judge or jury to see exactly what the witness saw when the incident or incidents in question occurred. It would then take very little time for it to be explained to the judge or jury and the accuracy of their understanding of it, represented by B's copy, should be very high. All players should be given a chance to look at other trios' constructions.

Iteration 2

But real life is much more difficult. In this iteration both A and B must have their backs to each other with their sets of bricks in front of them. Neither must be able to see what the other is building or has built. C once again watches and notes the time. In iteration 2, A makes a construction and when A has finished, A describes the construction to B who, *without asking any questions*, tries to build something similar with B's own bricks.

This iteration mirrors what would occur if witnesses were put on the stand and asked simply to tell their story in their own words. It is rare for the finder of fact (the judge or the jury) to ask any questions and so whoever is copying what the other person is telling them is not allowed to ask any questions or even indicate that they have understood. C notes how long it all takes and once again notes where any mistakes or inaccuracies occur. On this occasion inaccuracies usually relate to detail although the overall construction is pretty similar to the original.

Iteration 3

But what happens in the courtroom is even more complicated. In the courtroom an advocate asks questions of a witness, as a result of which questions and answers the finder of fact comes to certain conclusions. So, enter C in a new role. C is the advocate in iteration 3. C must still keep the time because that will still be necessary and it needs to be noted down at the end of each iteration. In addition, on this occasion, C must be placed with C's back to both the sets of bricks being constructed originally and the copy being made. A seating position rather like figure 5.1 is ideal; arrows show the direction in which the three characters should be facing, not the gender of the advocates.

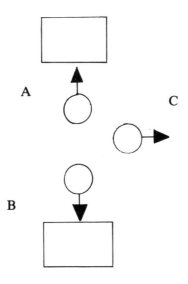

Figure 5.1   Seating arrangement for exercise 5 iteration 3

If C's back is close to the side of both A and B, C will hear more easily the answer to C's questions. Otherwise, it can become quite noisy in a room with more than three or four trios working on this exercise.

Either A or B will therefore make a construction and when finished will indicate to C to start the clock. If it is A who has made the construction then C will ask questions of A, as a result of the answers to which, B will copy A's construction. A is only allowed to answer the questions asked, just like a witness in court. B is not allowed to say whether B has understood or not, just like a judge or finder of fact in court. The advocate has to continue asking questions of the witness, listening to the replies, and trying to piece together in the advocate's own mind what understanding the judge or other finder of fact has come to.

When the advocate, C, has finished asking all the questions that C wishes to ask, C will then stop the clock and once again note down how long this exercise has taken. C will then look at the two constructions and note down the character of any mistakes or differences between them.

It will usually be found that iteration 3 took much longer than iteration 2, and that iteration 2 took much longer than iteration 1. Often iteration 3 takes *very* much longer than 2. The character of the mistakes which occur in iteration 3 are also often different from 2. Usually the details of the construction are very well executed but sometimes the overall picture is not as good.

On debriefing, the group leader should ask each trio whether their timekeeping has conformed to the picture just mentioned. Allowing a witness to tell the story in his or her own words takes *less* time than asking a large number of individual questions. Allowing a witness to tell the story in his or her own words usually also gives a better overview of the story and what the witness wants to say. However, it is often necessary to ensure that all the details are also given. Asking questions of the witness after the witness has told his or her own story on each issue will bring out any further details necessary. Thus a mixture of open questions for the witness followed by some closed, detailed questions, is the best combination with regard to both time taken and accuracy. All of this can be learned from the experience of carrying out this exercise and trainer feedback on how it went.

Another aspect of the system of evidence in court which it is important to learn from this exercise is the peculiar nature of the passage of information. It is not the judge or jury who ask questions so that *they* can understand what happened, it is a third party — the advocate — who asks all the questions of the witness. This is a highly inefficient and very strange system for satisfying the mind of someone else. However, this is how information on evidence passes in an adversarial court of law. The three iterations in the exercise make the point very clearly. The growing strangeness of each exercise assists in conveying this point in a very strong way.

The point should, however, be made that some magistrates, District Judges etc., will intervene and ask questions if they are unclear about the evidence, or feel the advocate has not done a full job. Also, some tribunals are run on an inquisitorial basis and tribunal members are expected to conduct an inquiry. Advocates under these circumstances should be careful to note when the tribunal is showing signs of wanting to ask questions.

To summarise, debriefing from this exercise involves explaining three important points about examination-in-chief. Information passes in a peculiar fashion in the courtroom. It is quicker to allow a witness to tell as much as possible of the story in his or her own words — and it is also very much more persuasive to hear the witness tell the story than to have it forced out by a large number of questions from the advocate. But details need to be mopped up by asking narrower questions subsequently.

Therefore, in relation to each issue to be dealt with by the witness, identified on the witness's statement or proof of testimony as in figure 2.1, the advocate should ask one open question followed by a few closed questions. The advocate should be following the witness's testimony on the reduced pages and the advocate should tick off each item as mentioned by the witness. Subsequently, each issue which the witness has not dealt with should be attended to by the advocate asking a more specific question in order for the witness to give information on each of those other issues. Each item can then be ticked off in turn.

The advocate should ask questions until each of those items is dealt with. If the witness still does not give the required information after a number of questions attempting to elicit this information, it may be necessary to try to obtain this information from another witness if that is possible or it may be that the required information will simply not come out at trial.

It is also important to note that in examination-in-chief the advocate should not 'lead' the witness, which means that the advocate should not direct the witness to answer any question in a particular way or suggest a particular answer to a question. The 'understanding blocks' game is a useful means of explaining all these elements of the examination-in-chief.

Exercise 6: the contours of the carpet

The next exercise was given its title because research shows that people have difficulty perceiving and remembering the colour of the carpet in the room in which they are sitting. At trial, however, there is a great pretence that people are capable of perceiving and remembering everything that they see. This is even more true for events which have been quite traumatic for some of the witnesses involved.

We make two types of conflicting suggestions about memory and perception in the course of advocacy. We pretend that everyone has complete memory recall and total perception at the time by asking questions about what people saw and what they remember they saw or heard. At the same time we pour scorn on the other side's witness who might claim to have seen and remembered something with great detail when we can show that this is very unlikely.

Here is an example of two sets of questions aiming in those two opposite directions. These questions are addressed to a witness who is a car rental agent:

First Advocate: So, as you have said Mr Smith you saw the defendant on 15 April 1992?

Witness: Yes I did.

First Advocate: And you are absolutely sure that it was the defendant?

Witness: Yes I am absolutely certain.

First Advocate: And what makes you so certain?

Witness: I have since looked at my records of that day and I have seen the name of the defendant on that computer printout.

Second Advocate (on cross-examination):   Well thank you, Mr Smith. You have told the court that it was definitely the defendant you hired the car to on that day?

Witness: Yes.

Second Advocate: Tell me, Mr Smith, about how many cars do you hire out yourself each day?

Witness: Oh, it differs, but on average about 10 cars a day.

Second Advocate: So in any one full week you would be hiring out about 70 cars?

Witness: Er, Yes.

Second Advocate: And in any one month you would be hiring out about 280 cars?

Witness: Yes.

Second Advocate: And in a year it would be close on 3,375 cars that you would hire out?

Witness: Yes.

Second Advocate: And you are telling this court, that you can clearly remember this man? (Sits down.)

Not only, then, do we have a very peculiar form of transmission of information in the courtroom but also we have a set of competing pretences about the character of information as it is presented. The art of the advocate is to use an understanding of both of these to the best advantage.

In order to develop this further, here is a set of questions which a trainer can modify for the purposes of a particular course. These questions are designed to show how little we perceive and remember, even in times of calm, of the world around us. The trainer should ask these questions for all the group participants to write down their answers individually, and then ask for the answers to be read back at the end of the exercise. It is useful not to leave a lot of time in between questions.

(a)   In feet, what is the length of the reception area in this building?

(b)   Describe the lighting in the reception area.

(c)   How many doors lead on to the reception area?

(d)   Close your eyes. Think of what colour shirt/blouse/jumper the person to your left is wearing (if there is no one to your left, then the person to your right). Without looking, write down the colour.

(e)   You are a juror, and you hear this verbal description of an incident:

One car, a red Nissan, was making a right turn. The other car, a Ford Escort, was coming from the other direction. The driver tried to stop, but the cars smashed into each other.

Please draw a diagram of the scene of the incident, based on this description. Locate the cars at the point of impact, and state their approximate speed just before the impact.

(f)   Did someone walk into this room during the training session? If so, please describe this person.

(g)   When a person is experiencing extreme stress as the victim of a crime, that person will have:

(i)   greater ability to perceive and recall the details of the event;
(ii)   the same ability to perceive and recall the details of the event as under normal conditions;
(iii)   reduced ability to perceive and recall the details of the event;
(iv)   greater ability to recall the details of the event, but less ability to perceive the details of the event.

(h)   If you are wearing a non-digital watch, do not look at it. Please state (i) whether it has numbers on it; (ii) its shape; (iii) Whether it has 'tick' marks to indicate minutes.

(i)   Do *not* look *up*. Is there a picture in the room? If so, what does the picture depict?

(j)   Do *not* look *up*. Are there any curtains in the room? If there are, what colour are they?

(k)   What were you doing exactly two weeks ago?

At the end of the exercise, when all the answers are read back, the trainer can dwell on the range of those answers. Course participants usually demand to know the *correct* answer for each question, but this is not the point. What is important is that all these potential witnesses had quite different perceptions and memories of the same item. This is also the case in the courtroom. Question (g) is answered correctly with answer (iii); but it is interesting how many people go for (iv).

Exercise 7: the gestatory period of the African elephant

The next stage in our educational process, having understood the nature of what goes on in the examination-in-chief, is to practise what is involved in asking questions in examination-in-chief. Asking such questions is not quite as easy as it looks on the films. We have already discussed the factual basis of questions in terms of the preparation of the proof of evidence of each witness. Each issue to be dealt with by the witness should probably be given a paragraph in the witness's proof and a reduced photocopy of each page of the testimony might well have a list of the two or three items from each paragraph which need to be brought out on examination-in-chief (see figure 2.1).

We have also already seen in the 'understanding blocks' exercise that a mixture of questions starting with open questions and ending up with some more closed questions is desirable. The next exercise allows the practice of questioning techniques without legal content, whilst concentrating very clearly on what is said by the witness and then devising further questions in order to bring out what is necessary.

When the author was studying A level English at school his teacher devised a method for beginning every essay, in order to practise the skill of linking issues within the body of the essay. Whether the essay was about 'The Intransigence of King Lear' or 'Male Characters in Jane Austen', each essay had to begin with the same sentence: 'The gestatory period of the African elephant is 18 months'. The essay then had to link this sentence in meaning with the main body of what the essay was intended to cover and then the essay could continue to develop in a normal fashion.

Out of this idea grew this next exercise. Participants should be divided into pairs and in each pair one person should be the questioner and the other person the witness. The 'witness' should think up some subject-matter about as far away from the gestatory period of African elephants as possible, such as transistor radios, cucumbers or catamaran sailing. The 'witness' will then tell the questioner the subject that the witness has thought of.

The questioner can then begin to ask questions of the witness. The first question must always be 'Do you know what the gestatory period of the African elephant is?' On the basis of the witness's answer to that question the questioner must link in the next question and following questions until the witness answers about the subject-matter previously stated (such as transistor radios, cucumbers or catamaran sailing).

A typical such exercise might go like this:

Witness: I want to answer on duck eggs.

Questioner: Okay. Do you know what is the gestatory period of the African elephant?

Witness: No I do not.

Questioner: Do you know anything about African elephants?

Witness: Very little.

Questioner: Do you know anything about any animals at all?

Witness: Yes I do know a little about some animals.

Questioner: Which animals are they?

Witness: Dogs and cats.

Questioner: So you don't know anything about any other domesticated animals?

Witness: No.

Questioner: And do you know anything about edible animals?

Witness: Yes I do.

Questioner: Do you know anything about edible fowls for example?

Witness: Yes, I do.

Questioner: What fowls do you know of, that one can eat?

Witness: Chickens, geese, pigeon and duck.

Questioner: So you know about ducks?

Witness: Yes.

Questioner: Do you know how they reproduce?

Witness: Yes, they produce duck eggs.

Questioner: Thank you very much.

Through playing this little party game the pair begin to get the feeling of asking and answering questions in the formal atmosphere of a courtroom. The 'witness' does not want to give immediately obvious answers usually and it is therefore a little more difficult to get to where the questioner wants. This adds to the fun and also helps the exercise itself.

After one run-thorugh, the pair should swap over roles and it is most important that both witness and questioner stand up when they are carrying out this exercise. Asking and answering questions whilst standing on one's feet somehow feels quite different from the atmosphere when one is sitting down at a table.

This exercise is very useful in encouraging the development of a cadence or rhythm in questions and just giving ideas for how to get started on a set of questions about different types of issues.

In terms of the subject-matter more often found in a legal trial, getting going on a line of questioning can often be helped by asking initially about the time, place, character or parties to the event. Provided that the date and time of the event were not in issue at the trial, an example would be:

Advocate: Do you remember the evening of 25th July?

Witness: Yes.

Advocate: Could you please tell the court what happened on that evening.

Exercise 8: *vive la différence*

The major 'difference' which is considered in this exercise is the differential effect of asking an open rather than a closed question. The difference is an essential element in the advocate's skill and must be understood right at the outset. An open question will elicit an 'open' answer allowing free-ranging thought and a number of possibilities. A closed question will allow only a very limited set of answers, sometimes only one.

One way of pointing this out is this exercise in which the course trainer asks two questions of the participants in the group.

The trainer should ask everyone to write down whatever answer comes into their heads to this question, 'How do you feel about cemeteries?' Encourage the participants to write down whatever answer they wish — sensible, sardonic, humorous or whatever, taking as much time as they need.

Then ask all the participants to answer this question, 'Do you think that there is an adverse effect on non-smokers' lungs as a result of someone else smoking in the same room as you?' Encourage the participants in the same way as before to answer exactly as they wish, once again being sardonic, sensible, humorous etc. and taking as much time as they need.

It is then interesting to ask all the members of the group to read out their answers to each of the two questions. Usually a range of answers appears in relation to cemeteries. People say they hate them, people say they love them, people say they have historic value, others say they are a waste of space, etc. There is both a wide-range of answer and length of answer given.

The answers to the question about smoking on the other hand are usually one word and are usually 'Yes'. The trainer can comment on this difference and how questioning should be phrased in order to allow or disallow a witness from being expansive or direct in answering.

Finally, playing a game similar to the gestatory period of the African elephant, it is possible to get a person with one view of cemeteries to encourage a person with a directly opposing view to mention and acknowledge the other person's view by asking questions in the same way as in the 'African elephant' exercise. This shows that even if as an advocate you start off by asking an open question and find that it has been too open for the answer that you wanted, it is still possible to find a way of suggesting to a witness the sort of answer you would have liked to have heard, without actually 'leading' the witness in an inappropriate way.

—————

Exercise 9: Olympics, royal weddings and embassy sieges

In this exercise the trainer or group leader picks out a member of the group in private before the session and agrees some subject-matter before the exercise starts. This should be something like the opening ceremony of the Olympic Games, a royal wedding or something fairly contemporary which would be common knowledge for most of the people in the group. One such example the author has often used is the siege of the Iranian Embassy — hence the peculiar title of the exercise.

The other members of the group are not aware of what is being referred to at the beginning. The group trainer begins asking a set of questions of the 'witness' in an illogical order. It is quite difficult for the other members of the group to follow what is being talked about. The witness only answers the questions asked. The group participants are asked to indicate when they know what it is which is being referred to and the trainer's objective is to try to make it as difficult as possible, through using a peculiar order, to understand and recognise the famous incident in question. So, in relation to the seige of the Iranian Embassy, the questioner might ask about what was going on in the front of the building, what was going on in the back of the building, where the witness was standing at the time etc., all in a way which could be confusing to the listener.

The objective of this exercise is to show how important it is to construct the examination-in-chief in such a way that a story is told to the judge or finder of fact. This means that questions of each witness must be asked in a logically ordered fashion so that the story can develop properly; and also that the order of witnesses is organised in such a way that the story can come out in a logical fashion. Even the most famous and well-known of events can become difficult to understand if not dealt with in this way. The advocate therefore must make careful decisions about the order in which to call witnesses and the order in which to ask questions of each witness. The chronological order of events is usually most effective, unless there are good reasons for an alternative.

—————

5.3   SUBMISSION OF NO CASE TO ANSWER

At the end of the prosecution case in a criminal trial it is possible for the defending advocate to submit to the court that the evidence adduced by the prosecution has not been sufficient to require the defence to bring its witnesses before the court. In other words an insufficient case has been made by the prosecution for a finding of guilt.

In a clear case the defence advocate should certainly proceed with such a submission. Where it is not so clear, it is always a fine judgment to be made on whether going through such a submission will not try the patience of the court. The advocate should therefore ensure that such a submission is entirely arguable and not to be brushed aside lightly.

The ingredients of such a submission are nicely portrayed in the skeleton map of the ingredients of law which would need to be proved for the prosecution's case to succeed. As the prosecution leads its case the defending advocate should mark where some evidence has been presented to prove each ingredient. Where evidence has not been produced on some of the ingredients necessary, this must be mentioned clearly to the court in a submission of no case to answer. Where evidence has been led on these issues but does not seem credible (as a result of the defending advocate's cross-examination of the witnesses) this also can be used as the basis of such a submission; but without the same force as a complete absence of evidence.

Presenting a submission of no case to answer is a useful exercise to go through in preparation of the defence of any criminal case. The new advocate should try a run-through of such a submission with colleagues prior to the trial. More experienced advocates should consider which issues are likely to be important for such a submission.

5.4   CONCLUSION

The basics of examination-in-chief have now been developed. The system of producing information between the triangle of questioner, witness and judge has been portrayed. The problems of human perception and memory have been expressed and the way in which these are used in court has been clearly shown. Methods of asking questions both in terms of being open or closed and of the order in which questions should be asked and the order of calling different witnesses have all been portrayed. Most of all it is important that examination-in-chief allows the witnesses to speak rather than the advocate. This may be changing in some courts where witness statements are taken as evidence-in-chief and only cross-examination becomes important. Where full examination-in-chief occurs, the advocate is there as a master or mistress of ceremonies, introducing and enhancing the other 'acts'. It is for the witnesses to give their evidence and in order to do so they must be allowed to tell a good deal of the story in their own words. Not only does this make their testimony more believable, it is also very much more efficient.

Chapter Six

Trial: Cross-examination, Re-examination and Closing

6.1 CROSS-EXAMINATION

For many new advocates the most worrying stage of a trial is not the opening speech, which they tend to feel is fairly straightforward, nor taking their own witnesses through examination-in-chief, which they tend to feel is not very different from a client or witness interview, but the cross-examination.

Cross-examination is usually portrayed as a duel of verbal and intellectual skills between advocate and witness, and advocate and opposing party, with the judge as referee between them. Cross-examination rarely reaches such heights of intellectual and emotional excitement and tension. It often (perhaps too often) is also part of a ritual whose basics can be very soon appreciated and learned by a little practice.

Neither does cross-examination have to be 'cross' in the sense of annoyed or aggressive. It is important, first of all, to understand the purposes and objectives of cross-examination. These are to cast doubt on, or undermine, or contradict the facts and views stated by the particular witness or views stated by other witnesses with which your side disagrees. It is important to note that your own side's witnesses in their examination-in-chief can equally be used to undermine, cast doubt on, or contradict the views stated by the other side. It is therefore not always essential to use a cross-examination of the other side's witnesses for this purpose. You have another means at your disposal, provided your own witnesses are able to bring out the issues you wish to address. This will already take some of the pressure off cross-examination.

In relation to some of the issues which arise in cross-examination a practising barrister:

610 (f)   must if possible avoid the naming in open court of third parties whose character would thereby be impugned;

(g)   must not by assertion in a speech impugn a witness whom he has had an opportunity to cross-examine unless in cross-examination he has given the witness an opportunity to answer the allegation;

(h)   must not suggest that a witness or other person is guilty of crime, fraud or misconduct or attribute to another person the crime or conduct of which his lay client is accused unless such allegations go to a matter in issue (including the credibility of the witness) which is material to his lay client's case and which appear to him to be supported by reasonable grounds.

Solicitors should also remember the effects of rule 14.02:

14.02   Principle

A solicitor must not make . . . an allegation which is intended only to insult, degrade or annoy the other side, the witness or any other person.

Commentary

1   This principle would also preclude a solicitor from making . . . an allegation which is merely scandalous.

2   In any litigation, a solicitor should, if possible, avoid the naming in open court of persons who are neither parties nor

witnesses if their characters would thereby be impugned. The court should be invited to receive in writing the names, addresses and other details of such third parties.

3   A solicitor should not, in a plea in mitigation, make . . . an allegation which is likely to vilify or insult any person, without first having satisfied himself that there are reasonable grounds for making the statement.

Exercise 10: destroying the myth

A practising barrister:

610   (e)   must not make statements or ask questions which are merely scandalous or intended or calculated only to vilify, insult or annoy either a witness or some other person.

An exercise which is intended to show the effects of being unpleasant to the other side's witness in court is one which can be carried out with a training group which has already been involved in some sessions of training on advocacy.

Select the most contentious of the people being trained and take this person aside prior to the next group meeting — preferably without any of the others observing. Warn this trainee that you will attempt to pick on some aspect of the trainee's behaviour in the early part of the seminar on cross-examination. Sometimes it can be helpful if this particular trainee enters the room a little late, as this will give a good opportunity to attack.

The trainer rounds on the particular trainee in a direct fashion, accusing the trainee of always being late, always indulging in private conversations, appearing not to wish to be involved in the seminar process or whatever. The trainee appears taken aback but does begin to argue. The trainer becomes even more direct and perhaps even a little unpleasant by standing on the dignity of the trainer's position.

Before getting to blows the trainer stops this conversation and is silent for a few moments.

On looking up it is clear that the entire group is ranged against the trainer and on behalf of the trainee who has been picked upon — even if they were rather testy about the trainee's behaviour previously. The two players will usually burst out laughing and that will release also some of the feeling of the audience if the act has gone well. It then becomes quite easy to point out how unpopular an advocate will become in the courtroom if the advocate uses the position of power on cross-examination of a witness and opens the witness to ridicule or other unpleasantness. Although the advocate might receive some of the answers preferred, the advocate will have lost the support of the court, especially if it is made up of a lay magistrate or jury. Once again the world of celluloid lets us down. Witnesses rarely break down in the witness-box and scream, 'Okay — I did it, I did it!', especially if they are simply witnesses of the good reputation of the defendant.

By creating an unpleasant atmosphere in the seminar room, the trainer has recreated the effect of this in the court and the group of those being trained do not quickly assume that cross-examination must annoy.

In fact, the best form of cross-examination, as will be seen later, will appear to agree almost entirely with the point of view of the witness, so much so that the witness feels taken 'hand in hand' with the cross-examiner.

Another point to recognise is that cross-examination of every witness is not obligatory. You do not *have* to cross-examine. You must think clearly before not doing so, but it may well be that it is not necessary in the circumstances of your case to cross-examine a particular witness. You should proceed with a cross-examination if you feel that not to do so would grant more credence to the witness than otherwise. But there are some circumstances where simply arguing the toss with a spirited and egotistical witness might get you nowhere. It might even serve to confirm the evidence which the witness has already given. In such circumstances you might decide that other evidence which you have already led or which you intend to lead in examination-in-chief will do the job for you.

Where, however, there is a direct conflict with a particular witness's testimony you almost certainly have a duty to at least put that conflict to the witness. Witnesses of fact in a criminal court will not know what other witnesses have said. It is your duty therefore to face the witness with the testimony of others and ask the witness to confirm or deny those points. Quite often, especially where an advocate knows that the witness will simply deny what is being put, this might take place in a ritualised form such as:

Advocate: So I put it to you, Police Constable Jones, that you next grabbed the defendant by the lapel and smashed him into the cell wall.

PC Jones: No, sir, I did not.

Advocate: I put it to you, PC Jones, that you then threw the defendant on to the floor and kicked him in the kidneys?

PC Jones: No, sir, I did not.

And so on.

In this way it is possible for an advocate to put a set of issues to the other side's witness to contradict, without necessarily going into the detail of the contrary allegations. The advocate's own case will then be disclosed more clearly on the defence setting forward their testimony in their examination-in-chief.

Similarly, if the other side's witness is not relevant to your case it is not necessary to cross-examine. This could occur, for example, where a witness has testified as to quantum of damage in a car accident. If you are not disputing the quantum, but only your client's liability, you can forego cross-examination.

So, it is possible not to cross-examine. It is also possible to cross-examine simply in a ritualistic form by presenting competing testimony for the other side's witness to reject. Neither does cross-examination have to be long in order to be effective. Quite often the most devastating cross-examination can be a fairly short build-up, rather like in boxing with one blow to the body followed by a quick blow to the chin. The advocate can then sit down feeling that the witness has been shaken a little without necessarily needing to proceed with a knock-out. In fact, many witnesses learn quickly how to deal with the advocate's questions and get better at it as they spend time in the witness-box. Also, the patience of the judge or jury can be lost if an advocate keeps plugging away at the same sort of issues without seeming to get anywhere, or appears to be dealing with items which are not obviously relevant to the way the trial has progressed. All of these factors need to be considered carefully before embarking on cross-examination.

The great worry about cross-examination for the advocate is that it appears to be completely unprepared and based on a set of spur-of-the-moment decisions having just heard the examination-in-chief of that witness. This also is not really an accurate picture of what occurs. In most civil cases the advocate will have a very good idea of what facts or allegations are likely to be presented to the court by the other side well before the trial. Discovery of documents, sight of witness statements under the new rules of court, the defence and other pleadings themselves and informal information culled from dealings with the other side should all help to provide the advocate with an awareness of what is likely to occur. The defence in a criminal trial will also be pretty much aware of the witness statement which the prosecution witnesses are going to give in evidence. Only the prosecution in a criminal trial is not aware of the likely defence, unless it be an alibi, which is going to be given by defence witnesses at trial. Even in such cases there is a finite set of likely types of defence which appear to recur with some regularity in the criminal courts.

Being aware of what the other side's witnesses are likely to produce means that it is possible to construct beforehand the sorts of questions which one might wish to use for cross-examination. These also will always relate to the main issues in the case and reviewing the map outline of law and fact should therefore be a helpful guide, whatever the case involves.

It is good practice to take careful notes of testimony given by the other side's witnesses and at the same time as doing so it is helpful to highlight, or asterisk or underline, areas on which you feel cross-examination may be necessary. By leaving a margin against these notes you can add comments such as XX (cross-examination), FS (final speech) or IC (examination-in-chief). This noting down of the other side's testimony, whilst applying your mind to how you might cross-examine on it, is one of the hardest parts of advocacy, although certainly not recognised as such in most of the films, or even the textbooks!

To summarise, then, we have discussed whether you should cross-examine at all, how long cross-examination should be, and what elements of the other side's case it should involve, i.e., those items which you need to contradict in order to substantiate your own case. We can now turn to the way in which you should cross-examine.

6.1.1   The magic fence

It is therefore time to do some practical work on how to cross-examine. But before we get down to this exercise, it is useful to conceptualise what it is we are asking cross-examiners to do.

In cross-examination the aim of the advocate is to suggest something to the finder of fact — a judge or jury. That 'something' will usually be that the witness's evidence on examination-in-chief is in some way uncertain, unreliable or incorrect. Note that in criminal trials it is necessary for the defence only to cast 'a reasonable doubt' in order to reach the standard of 'beyond unreasonable doubt'. A larger level of doubt is necessary in civil trials where the burden of proof is on a balance of probabilities.

You should think of the issue you are suggesting as fenced in by a circle (see figure 6.1). Your objective with the witness is to approach slowly, little by little, the fence around that issue from a few different directions thereby delineating to the court the issue itself, without necessarily coming within the ring fence around the issue. Thus, the broken lines in figure 6.1 each show a set of questions

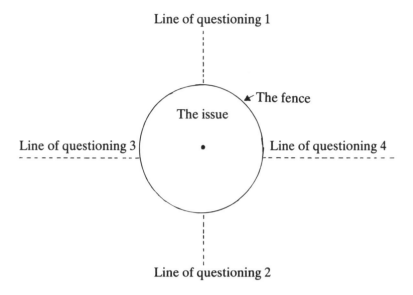

Figure 6.1 Map of cross-examination

which stop just outside the boundary of the fenced-in circle. If you were suggesting to a witness that the witness may not have been able to see a car crash in which your client was involved, the sorts of questions you might ask might go like this:

Advocate: Thank you, Mr Jenkins. I have listened carefully to what you have said to the court already and I would just like to ascertain clearly whether my understanding of what you have said is correct. Now, you were standing on the side of the road?

Jenkins: Yes.

Advocate: You were facing up the road towards Wembley Stadium, because you were walking in that direction?

Jenkins: Yes that's right.

Advocate: And you were walking along with your friends?

Jenkins: Yes.

Advocate: It was about 7 o'clock at night?

In that sequence the advocate has followed through a set of questions leading up to the fence, and the last question is beginning a further series, diagrammatically, starting from another point — noted as point 2 on figure 6.1. Each of the questions asked is short and simple. It invites the answer yes rather than a negative answer. Yet it begins to cast doubt on what the witness says that he saw, if he was facing in the opposite direction to the accident, if it was beginning to get dark, and if he was talking with friends.

Unlike in examination-in-chief you do not ask *any* open questions which would allow the witness to develop the story in his or her own words. You ask only very closed questions determining a particular response. You also want to teach the witness simply to answer in one or two words and basically to agree with what you are saying. After a few lines of questioning it will be fairly clear to everyone else in the court, perhaps apart from the witness, what is being suggested. Four 'lines of questioning' are displayed in figure 6.1.

Exercise 11: hand in hand

For the purposes of this exercise the trainer should construct a factual situation of the kind to be faced by the group being trained in their likely first forays in advocacy. It could deal with a motor accident as above, or with seeing a bank robbery, or hearing a child's screams or something of the sort. The group should be asked for each member to construct a series of questions either on paper or in their minds querying whether the witness could really have seen what the witness has said. It is then a good idea to ask one or two of them to stand up and try to take you as the witness through some cross-examination based on those questions.

The first objective of this exercise is simply to construct a series of closed questions leading towards a discernible goal but not actually asking the issue itself: 'Did you really see the incident?', which could be the 'one question too many'. The second objective is to organise the form of the questions so that the witness's likely answers will be yes. Thus the witness will feel taken along 'hand in hand' up to the fence.

6.1.2 Asking the one question too many

An amusing, if almost certainly totally apocryphal, story is told about a cross-examination in which the advocate asks the 'one question too many' and actually goes inside the ring fence. The scene of the case is a rugby football match and the defendant is accused of biting off the ear of the victim during a fracas on the field of play. A bystander witness is in the witness-box and he has just testified that he saw the defendant bite off the victim's ear. The advocate is working on the theory that the players with the ball at the time were located in the opposite direction, from the point of view of where the witness was standing, to the place at which the fracas between defendant and victim was occurring and therefore the witness could not have seen the incident. These were the questions the advocate asked:

Advocate: So, Mr Witness, where were you standing at the time?

Witness: I was standing on the side of the playing-field on the halfway line.

Advocate: And what was happening on the field of play?

Witness: Well player A passed back to player B, B had just passed to player C and C had just passed to player A.

Advocate: And whereabouts was this occurring?

Witness: All of this was to the right of me going towards the red goalposts.

Advocate: Good. Now where was the defendant at the time?

Witness: The defendant was standing about 20 yards to my left.

Advocate: And the victim?

Witness: The victim was in about the same position as the defendant.

Advocate: Let's go back to the field of play now. You said that C passed back to A and then what happened?

Witness: Well A then made a run for a try and was tackled by X.

Advocate: Well, I put it to you, Mr Witness, that you were so involved in watching what was going on in the field of play that you could not possibly have seen the defendant bite off the ear of the victim.

(This of course is the one question too many.)

Witness: Yes, that is absolutely true, but I did see him spit it out.

Thus it can be shown that it is not a good idea to ask a question which allows the witness into the charmed circle. The witness will only deny everything that you, the advocate, have been building up to, as you approach the fence.

6.1.3   Form and cadence

In constructing a line of questioning on cross-examination it is important to pay attention to the most efficient form for such questions and also the rhythm in which such questions are asked, and then answered. If the objective of the cross-examining advocate is to take the witness 'hand in hand' then it is necessary that the witness should continue, as far as possible along the line of questioning, to answer the questions positively, in the affirmative. In other words, you want the witness to agree with you.

The best way to do this is to cut up the factual area which you are addressing in your questions into very small pieces, starting with a set of questions to which you know the witness has already given their answers. This approach has already been portrayed in 6.1.1 where the ability of Mr Jenkins, the witness, to have seen a road accident is being slowly undermined. Further questions within the same cross-examination might appear something like this:

Advocate: It was about 7 o'clock at night?

Jenkins: Yes, between 7 and 7.15.

Advocate: And just remind us please what month was this?

Jenkins: It was late September.

Advocate: Yes, and the evenings were drawing in.

Jenkins: Yes.

Advocate: Do you remember, are there any lampposts along Wembley Hill Road?

Jenkins: Oh yes, there certainly are.

Advocate: And were the lights on, on the lampposts?

Jenkins: Oh, I am not sure.

The idea, therefore, is to continue to take the witness along hand in hand with these short questions. At some point you might well ask a question, just like the last one, to which you do not know the answer, or at least do not know how the witness is going to answer. This is not such a problem. The advocate has already suggested to the court implicitly that it was getting dark. If Jenkins testifies that the lights were on, then the court would know that it probably was dark. If Jenkins testifies that the lights were not on, the advocate has already suggested that it was getting dark and that answer could suggest less visibility than if the lights had been on. Finally, Jenkins actually answers that he does not remember. This answer is equally good for the advocate because it suggests that if Mr Jenkins does not remember this he might well not have remembered everything else he says he saw accurately. Most of all, the witness is being educated into agreeing with the advocate and answering fairly shortly in a sort of rhythm. When one watches experienced advocates involved in this style of cross-examination it sometimes feels almost as if the witness is mesmerised by the court atmosphere and questions, and is grateful simply to agree, rather than be attacked.

6.1.4   Confrontation

All of this is not to say that there are not times when witnesses must be confronted either with untruth or with the possibility of their own misapprehension or poor memory. We have already considered the 'ritual' in respect of Police Constable Jones (above) as one form of the confrontational rather than confirmatory approach. We will now go on to look at other occasions on which this approach becomes necessary. Where the whole objective of your case necessitates undermining the integrity or believability of a witness, it will clearly be necessary to do something different from simply getting the witness to agree with you. Although it may be possible to show up their own lack of credibility by getting them to agree with sets of contrary propositions, at some point you may well have to confront them with that difference. Similarly where, in order to prove your case, it is necessary to attack not the witness's personal integrity but how believable is the story which the witness has told, or particular parts of that story, it will be necessary to expose this lack of credibility to the judge or jury. Even here, it is possible to use the 'silver tongue' approach rather than anything directly confrontational. But the silver-tongued advocate needs to be ready to move over to a more direct approach if the witness turns from positive to negative.

Even in cases where you may be directly disagreeing with parts of the witness's testimony, it will be very unlikely that you will disagree with everything the witness has said. You can still therefore pull out some levels of agreement in relation to almost every witness.

It should be noted that although you need to 'put' your case on matters in issue to the other side's witnesses it is not your job, on cross-examination, to go through the entire story told by the witness. You can pick and choose where to attack and you can afford to be as selective as you wish. There is no need to deal with the testimony in chronological order, or in the order in which it was given, although sometimes such an approach can be quite devastating if it is your intention to counter absolutely everything the witness has said. Mostly, you will want to carry out a set of small guerrilla raids on specific areas of testimony and then run back to the cover of your own battle lines.

Exercise 12: under the microscope

Since the major aim of cross-examination is to cast some doubt, or even just a little cold water, on the evidence of the other side, one particular approach is often very helpful for this. This is the approach used in the exercise 'under the microscope'. In this exercise the seminar leader notes a set of obvious truisms prior to the session. These should be of the sort that it is possible to argue with, but unlikely that anyone would try to do so. A few examples are:

(a)   Night follows day.

(b)   William Shakespeare wrote the works of Shakespeare.

(c)   The Judaeo-Christian Bible is principally divided into the Old and New Testaments.

(d)   Ice is a solid form of water.

It will be evident that although the above are pretty much accepted facts, it is still possible to question their validity. In order to carry out this exercise those attending the seminar are invited to think up a set of questions in relation to any of these 'truisms' which would tend to put the item 'under a microscope'. Looking closely at it would tend to suggest that it may not be quite as obviously true as previously seen to be the case. The seminar leader can act as the 'witness', whilst in turn a number of members of the seminar can stand up and cross-examine the seminar leader on the item in question. By magnifying the fact out of all proportion, the effect is to suggest its unreliability. This is not very different from the familiar rhetorical device of *reductio ad absurdum*.

So, on the item 'night follows day' it would be possible to suggest that in fact day followed night, on the item that Shakespeare wrote 'his' works it would be possible to suggest knowledge of the literature doubting this. On ice being a solid form of water it could quite easily be suggested that a chemical change occurs rather than a physical change and so the molecular structure of ice and its chemical properties could well be different from water. All that is necessary is to raise the slightest doubt by such questions.

A further finesse on this exercise is to encourage the seminar group itself to come up with a set of absolute facts and then get them and the seminar leader to find ways of questioning these.

The objective of this exercise is to show that there is not a fact in the universe which is not questionable in some way when placed under the microscope. If this is correct then the sort of facts which are produced in court in evidence are certainly susceptible to being questioned in this manner.

It may be worth considering a practical example. Dr Jones testifies that she left her house at 8.26 in the morning on the day in question. This becomes of some importance since the sequence of events in the incidents in question in the trial may well be affected by the exact time at which Dr Jones left her house. On cross-examination you are quite concerned lest your questioning has the effect of strengthening what she has said. So, let's have a go at her:

Advocate: Dr Jones, you have testified that you left your house at 8.26 on the day in question?

Dr Jones: Yes.

Advocate: In the courtroom we have heard a number of conflicting stories about the time and sequence of the accident, so that it is quite important to be sure that we have got this time right.

Dr Jones: Yes, I am sure.

Advocate: Do you always leave the house at exactly the same time?

Dr Jones: No, not exactly — but about that time.

Advocate: When you say, 'about that time', within what sort of range of time would you normally leave the house?

Dr Jones: Well, from about quarter past eight to about half past eight.

Advocate: And your habits in leaving the house are always very regular whatever happens?

Dr Jones: Yes.

Advocate: Even if there is a hiccup over you or another member of the family being ready in time?

Dr Jones: Well, yes, within reason.

Advocate: Could you tell the court how you know it was 8.26 when you left the house on that day?

(The advocate is, of course, shooting in the dark here without being absolutely clear of the answer — but this is not quite as dangerous as it looks.)

Dr Jones: I looked at my watch immediately after the accident occurred, because I knew I had to get to the surgery by 8.45 and so I could count back quite easily to the time that I had left.

Advocate: So you were just calculating by working backwards from the time of the accident?

Dr Jones: Yes.

At this point, the advocate could quite happily just keep away and sit down or carry on with cross-examining on another issue because the suggestion has already been made to the court that the exactness of the time stated could be in question. Alternatively, the advocate could hammer away further by putting the testimony under the microscope, in this way.

Advocate: Could you just describe to the court what sort of procedure you go through when you leave the house in the morning.

Dr Jones: Well I look for my case, fetch the newspaper, kiss the children goodbye and shout up to my husband.

Advocate: In that order?

Dr Jones: And then I close the door and walk towards the car.

Advocate: Is it a long drive that you walk down?

Dr Jones: No, about 8 to 12 yards.

Advocate: So, 24 to 36 feet?

Dr Jones: Yes.

The advocate would then go on to question about opening the doors of the car, getting in to the car, setting the choke, starting the car etc. Provided the judge had not tired of this line of questioning it would soon become very clear that all of this procedure could certainly take more than the time which the good doctor had counted backwards from the time of the accident.

To summarise, then, this particular technique involves finding a fact, even the most straightforward one, and just beginning to loosen the soil underneath it a little by undermining the suggestions made by the witness. This particular approach works because witnesses know that they must rely on a certain amount of commonly accepted knowledge in order to give their testimony. It is this level of common knowledge and blind acceptance of that knowledge which allows the advocate to do a little bit of undermining of the area.

––––––––––

Exercise 13: the gold high jump medal

This is the last exercise for our cross-examination section and is intended to teach the importance of inferences and to loosen up the cross-examining approaches of new advocates. When the author acts as seminar leader he 'testifies' to the class that he was awarded the gold high-jump medal at the last Olympic games. He points out that if a direct question is asked on this issue he will repeat that testimony. However, any indirect question (which would tend to show that it is rather unlikely that he did win the gold high-jump medal) would be answered honestly.

The objective of this exercise is to persuade advocates to concentrate in cross-examination on the inferences which may be drawn from a piece of testimony rather than the testimony itself. In similar fashion to the magic fence around testimony this allows the advocate to chip away at the inferences which lead from the testimony without having to attack the crux.

A good way of carrying out this exercise is to encourage the seminar members to think up one question only or at the most two questions, one leading on from the other, to ask. The seminar leader then goes around the class seeing what people ask. As soon as someone asks the question, 'But did you really win the gold high-jump medal?', the answer always will be yes.

The sort of questions which are quite useful in undermining the testimony about the gold high-jump medal by going at inferences to be drawn from it have in the past included:

Question 1:   Where did these Olympics take place?

Answer: In my back garden in Wembley.

Question 2:   What height did you jump when you won?

Answer: About 3 feet 3 inches.

Question 3:   Who were the other competitors?

Answer: There was my 10-year-old son and the neighbours' dog called Spot.

Question 4:   How much training did you have for this event?

Answer: I did have double Weetabix on the morning concerned.

And so on.

Very soon, even those who feel nervous about the exercise of cross-examination can enter into the spirit of this game and realise how much easier it is to attack an inference than a fact itself. They also become a little more adept at asking one-line questions, which is a somewhat different cadence to that suggested above. These one-liners are the body-blows of cross-examinations. No witness is really capable of thinking through every possible answer to questions of this nature aimed not at the evidence itself but at external inferences to be drawn from that evidence. Witnesses can therefore not prepare themselves easily for these questions.

6.1.5   Summary and conclusion

A number of techniques of cross-examination have been portrayed in this section. We have first of all shown that it is not essential always to cross-examine and that even if you do need to do so it certainly does not need to be aggressive. The best cross-examination takes the witness with the advocate and works with the grain of both witness and testimony and not against that grain.

It is useful to set up a 'magic fence' around the issue which you are attacking, asking sets of questions approaching the same issue from different directions. Encouraging your witnesses to fall into the habit of answering with one or two words to each question is useful in taking them along the lines you intend.

It is necessary sometimes to confront a witness with opposing facts, statements or ideas, but even this does not have to be done in an unpleasant manner. Giving the witness two possibilities and asking for a choice between them can be a 'heads I win tails you lose' set-up if organised properly.

It is possible to direct attention to a particular issue by magnifying it out of all proportion or else to ignore the crux of the issue and to attack inferences which might be drawn from it. Cross-examination can be planned to some extent. It need not be decided on the spur of the moment and there are a certain number of basic routines which are useful to try.

In order to undermine someone's testimony it is not necessary to attack everything they say and it is not necessary to do it in a particular order. You can pick and choose your order and even move back and forth between different issues. However, you should ensure that what is understood by the court in listening to the effect of your cross-examination is coherent. All in all, cross-examination is not the terror that it appears in cinematic or television mythology. It can be brilliant, but is often simply painstaking attention to specific and important details alone.

6.2 RE-EXAMINATION

You can only undertake re-examination when the cross-examination of your witness by the other side has brought out new areas of factual testimony which were not covered in your examination-in-chief. Where this has occurred, it is possible to go over the new facts with the witness in order to set out for the court a fuller, or different, picture than was available as a result of the other side's cross-examination.

Because re-examination is possible, the 'one question too many' (see 6.1.2) is often not quite such a serious factor as portrayed above. In other words, if cross-examination has deeply undermined your witness by not allowing your witness to give testimony that the witness wishes to give, it is sometimes possible on re-examination to reassert those issues.

The techniques of re-examination are not very different from those involved in examination-in-chief and the skills and exercises set out there for drawing out the witness's testimony and resubstantiating your point will equally be useful in re-examination.

6.3   CLOSING SPEECH

Criminal courts and civil courts differ in the ability of the respective parties to make closing speeches. In the magistrates' court, for example, only the defence make a closing speech, unless the prosecution have reserved their right to come back on questions of law if raised by the defence. In some courts both parties make closing speeches. The rules of tribunals also differ. In this section we will look at some of the special characteristics of the closing speech in whatever circumstances it is given.

The Bar's code of conduct states:

> 1.7   It is the duty of prosecuting counsel to assist the court at the conclusion of the summing-up by drawing attention to any apparent errors or omissions of fact or law.

The closing speech by its nature is the last piece of representation which will be heard by the court from a particular advocate or a particular side. It is therefore a crucial element in representing the client's interests. The first and last things that anyone reads or sees or hears have more effect than those in the middle. This is known as the 'primacy and recency effects'. The recency effect will apply to the closing speech.

The content elements of the closing speech can be divided into two sections: one part which can be prepared before the hearing and the second part which cannot. At this point in time, the advocate will know not only what evidence the advocate wished the court to hear from each side but also what evidence actually did emerge. The bulk of a closing speech which can be mapped out in outline prior to the hearing is a restatement of the issues in contest between the two sides and the evidence which you as advocate expect to be adduced by your side in relation to them. This is once again the road-map of law and fact of the trial which will have been set out in your preparation prior to the day of the hearing. In addition to this basis it will be necessary to make some further points which are likely to be related to the same issues. The further points which could arise will be your reactions to any evidence which undermines your case.

This can be mentioned in the closing speech and conflicting evidence from your own side may be set clearly against it.

Conversely, your own witnesses may not have come up to proof and it may be that there is something that you wanted or expected them to say which did not emerge. You might then be in the position where you need to reconstruct your approach to that issue, based on the evidence which was heard. Often it is possible to pray in aid evidence given by the other side in order to prove the same issue, even if that evidence was given on cross-examination.

Your basic aim, then, in a closing speech is to summarise the same crucial issues which appeared in your overall road-map of the case, but this time in the light of the evidence which has actually been given in court. You may use any of the evidence from either side to argue or suggest the case that you are leading.

6.3.1 Dealing with the law

In some courts this will also be the time to address questions of law. You may have to argue about how your case fits in with a decided case or line of cases in order to achieve the particular solution you desire. This might well mean distinguishing the facts of your case from a particular line of cases and allying it with the facts and decisions of another line of cases. Although this activity is much closer to the sort of arguments that occur at the appellate level, some cases will be decided on this basis even at trial.

Cases which go to trial tend to involve a major disagreement between the two sides. Sometimes there is little disagreement on the facts but there is some uncertainty about the law. Quite often there is disagreement on both. The skills involved in distinguishing cases and arguing about which way your case should be decided are principally the fundamental, intellectual case-handling skills which are taught at undergraduate level, in the CPE or in the legal practice course for the Law Society finals. They are often what is referred to as 'thinking like a lawyer'. These are the skills most often tested in examination-type problems at university and in the CPE. Now, is the time to use those skills in presenting not simply both sides of the question but also why your client should win.

As with everything else in advocacy you should attempt to make the exposition of the law clear without ignoring any real complexity. Refer to a specific case or cases, ensure that the other side and the court know which case you are referring to and if possible have a copy of it, then take the court through as much detail of the facts of that case as is necessary for your argument. Do not assume that the court is aware of even the most 'trite' law, unless the court assures you that there is no need for you to take that case of that argument any further. Having explained the facts in brief, so far as is necessary, of the precedent to which you refer, you should relate it clearly to the facts of your case and then move on to any other cases. Remember that it is your obligation to the court not to hide from the court those cases which are against you. It is then your duty to the client to distinguish clearly between them. If possible allow the court the opportunity to ask you questions on your arguments of law. Hypothetical cases are unlikely to be put to you at the trial-court level but if the argument is complex you should think through some possible hypotheticals in your preparation of the argument. None of the legal issues should be a major surprise for you since they should all be part of your preparation well prior to the hearing.

6.3.2   Last-chance reprieve

Your closing speech is your last chance to get across particular ideas and it is worthwhile doing so effectively but not at too much length. What is too long will really depend upon what has gone before. As always with advocacy, you should pay very close attention to the atmosphere in the court and the reactions of the judge. The best closing speech will be worthless if it loses the attention and the concentration of those whom you are trying to persuade. Always remember that this is not an exercise in a vacuum. You are trying to persuade real people about a real person's, or business entity's, case. Putting your arguments in a human, rather than a distant, objective style will be useful for particular fora. Where more senior judges are present and deciding the case, a more 'objective', professional or distant style may be more appropriate.

Chapter Seven

Plea in Mitigation

In a criminal court where the defendant has either pleaded guilty or been found guilty after pleading not guilty, it will be necessary for the advocate for the defence to make a plea in mitigation of the offence. The plea in mitigation is sometimes characterised as an emotional and personal pleading by the advocate on behalf of the unfortunate defendant. It can certainly be this in the appropriate case. Such cases might be appropriate where a first offender appears to have got into trouble by mistake and bad fortune rather than by evil intention.

However, a plea in mitigation does not need to be emotional and this might well be inappropriate either for the offence concerned, the offender or the character of the court. Where the offence is socially offensive, or the defendant has a very bad character, the job of the advocate in mitigation is to find as many positive aspects as possible to set before the court. This can include the otherwise good works of the defendant. It can also include a logical argument on why one form of sentence would be more rational in the circumstances, or compared with other sentences in allied areas of law. In none of these cases is it necessary to appeal to emotion or sentiment where such feelings might not be available to be reached.

Quiet often, in court, it is clear that a plea in mitigation is simply a ritual and is hardly thought about by the advocate and hardly listened to by the court. A plea should always be personal and direct in relation to the crime and the offender so that it will not become part of the norm. Each case is clearly individual and this is the time to recognise that fact.

Although it may be difficult in certain circumstances the advocate should be careful not to overstress the problems of the defendant, especially if the victim or society have suffered very much more from the offence concerned than the defendant had suffered from society. Such over-egging of the pudding can have exactly the opposite effect to that which is intended. A measure of balance must be struck at the same time as a show of clear partisanship.

In the light of the above comments it will be clear that there can be no overarching formula for addressing a plea in mitigation. Indeed the advocate should be at some pains to construct an individual argument or set of arguments specific to the case in hand.

Exercise 14: great villains of all time

A useful exercise for those involved in criminal work looks at the position of some of the world's greatest villains. In this exercise those attending the seminar are asked to construct a plea in mitigation for people such as Judas Iscariot, Adolf Hitler, Ghengis Khan, Joseph Stalin.

The seminar members are each asked to choose their 'favourite' villain and to construct a plea in mitigation for the atrocities they committed. They should be advised to find three positive aspects of the life of the individual concerned or three mitigating factors for the person's bad behaviour. So, in relation to Adolf Hitler the plea in mitigation might include the fact that he was born out of wedlock, was a member of an impoverished working class (a painter and decorator) and was blessed with unfortunate physical features. In relation to Joseph Stalin it might be said that he was very kind to his mother, set up charities for orphans and was prepared to fight against Adolf Hitler. Each of the themes should be developed by the seminar participants into a speech which should last approximately five minutes.

The objective of the exercise is to show that having prepared a plea in mitigation for such villains it will not be that difficult ever again to construct a plea in mitigation for defendants in court. Five minutes is quite a long time to speak in favour of some of the above villains and it could well stretch the imagination of those involved to find something to say in their favour.

A plea in mitigation is the only act of advocacy which an advocate representing a defendant who is pleading guilty will have to undertake. Time should be spent with the defendant in advance to discover anything which might be said to the defendant's advantage. Facts in mitigation do not often sit well with the sort of facts lawyers want to discover from their clients in relation to defending the client on a plea of not guilty. Where a client is intending to plead not guilty, it is still incumbent on the lawyer to try to ascertain such facts as are necessary for mitigation, prior to the hearing. There may well not be an adequate opportunity to take further instructions from the client between the decision of the court and the time for the plea in mitigation.

The Bar's conduct code states:

1.8   In relation to sentence, prosecuting counsel:

(a)   should not attempt by advocacy to influence the court with regard to sentence; if, however, a defendant is unrepresented it is proper to inform the court of any mitigating circumstances about which counsel is instructed;

(b)   should be in a position to assist the court if requested as to any statutory provisions relevant to the offence or the offender and as to any relevant guidelines as to sentence laid down by the Court of Appeal;

(c)   should bring any such matters as are referred to in (b) above to the attention of the court if in the opinion of prosecuting counsel the court has erred;

(d)   should bring to the attention of the court any appropriate compensation, forfeiture and restitution matters which may arise on conviction, for example, pursuant to sections 35 to 42 of the Powers of Criminal Courts Act 1973 and the Drug Trafficking Offences Act 1986;

(e)   should draw the attention of the defence to any assertion of material fact made in mitigation which the prosecution believes to be untrue; if the defence persists in that assertion, prosecuting counsel should invite the court to consider requiring the issue to be determined by the calling of evidence in accordance with the decision of the Court of Appeal in *R* v *Newton* (1983) 77 Cr App R 13.

Chapter Eight

Mopping-up Operations

Although your job as a representative of your client's case has almost finished there are still a number of other items to be dealt with before you can leave the courtroom let alone the courthouse. These include noting the decision, dealing with costs, considering the question of appeals and advising the client. A number of these issues have already been covered in brief in chapter 4, and they are much more important in our current context.

8.1 NOTING THE JUDGMENT

It is always a good idea to take a fairly full note of the judgment given by the court. In certain instances, such as at the Crown Court, a full version will be taken down by the court recorder or by some other recording device. In the magistrates' court the clerk would usually note the decision clearly. In other courts written decisions may subsequently appear. But in all cases you may need to make up your own mind and advise the client on what the judge has said well in advance of a written, transcribed or other version of what was said. In some small way, it may still be possible to have some effect on changing the decision or parts of it even at this stage. For all these reasons a written note is essential.

Experience suggests what elements in the judgment especially to look for, but these will often relate to the other issues to be dealt with in this chapter. Therefore anything which might affect costs or appeals should be listened to carefully and noted. This noting procedure is even more important if it is likely to be the job of your side to draw up the judgment in the court office.

As mentioned above in relation to preliminary hearings, such notes are sometimes used by the courts in order to decide what the judge actually did say and did decide in a particular case. They may therefore have even greater use than simply for your own pragmatic purposes.

8.2   COSTS

The costs of a trial are likely to be substantial and therefore any issue of costs must be fought extremely hard and thought through carefully beforehand. Frequently, in civil cases, the costs of the trial and the preparation for it can far outstrip the damages at issue between the parties. Although this can be seen as a major indictment of any system of justice, it is a fact of life which lawyers must deal with.

Preparation on questions of costs can certainly be organised in advance of the trial and discussed with colleagues to determine what is likely to be reasonable in the event of winning or losing. The file should be reviewed carefully to see whether any quirks of practice by the other side would change the normal allocation of costs. Some of these issues might only come out on a full taxation, but more major decisions might be available to be made by the judge in the action itself.

The costs issue is not minor and can in the final analysis be the most important element for the client — even those clients who previously stated that their case was 'a matter of the greatest principle'. Dealing with the question of costs and reacting to any suggestions from the other side should be an automatic response of the advocate at the end of the hearing rather than a tired after-thought from an exhausted winner or loser.

8.3 APPEALS

In your preparation for the hearing you will also have noted the possibility of appeal. You may well have taken this into account from the point of view of a successful, as well as an unsuccessful, advocate. In many cases it will not be necessary for you to do anything immediately at the end of a hearing with regard to an appeal. But you will almost certainly need to be in a position to advise the client on this subject immediately after the hearing whether you have succeeded on behalf of your client or not. You therefore need to know the position clearly.

Where it is necessary to make some intervention, or possible to ask for some intervention, regarding an appeal immediately after receiving the judgment and discussing the question of costs, you should be ready to do so. This might include asking for a case stated, or for notes to be preserved, or even asking for leave to appeal from the trial judge or judges themselves. Where nothing needs to be said in court it may still be useful to organise the preparation of papers or making appointments with the court office after leaving the courtroom.

It is quite difficult to consider and keep in mind this issue as an advocate, having been victorious. But you still need to be aware of the possibility so that you can defend against its occurrence if necessary. If acting as the prosecutor the court can also sometimes call on you to give advice on the details of the possibility of appeal. You should therefore be ready to do so.

The barristers' code also states:

> 6.2   If his client pleads guilty or if convicted, defence counsel should see his client after he has been sentenced in the presence of his professional client or his representative. He should then express orally any provisional view he may have formed as to the prospects of a successful appeal. In any event counsel should inform his lay client that he will furnish written advice to the professional client as soon as he can and in any event within 21 days.

8.4   KEEPING THE CLIENT WITH YOU

As soon as your hearing is finished the most important person to get
to is the client. So often advocates spend time immediately after the
hearing with other advocates or lawyers whilst the client waits
mystified somewhere behind, and sometimes in the cells. The
elements of the decision may seem fairly obvious to you but will still
probably not have been understood by your client. The importance
of the occasion often makes it quite difficult for the client to
appreciate what has occurred and what is now going to happen.
Where the case has not gone totally in the way your client would
have wished it is even more important to explain to the client why
you feel this has occurred and what exactly is going to happen now.
This means that 'We've won' or 'We've lost' are not sufficient
expositions of what is likely to have occurred in the courtroom.

There may be a large number of items which have mystified the
client and which the client has not had the opportunity to ask you
about. They may, in the event, be totally irrelevant to the decision;
but the client does not know this. You must therefore be at the
client's disposal to answer any such questions the client may have
resulting from the hearing.

Most courts have one or two small consulting rooms where you can
talk privately with your client. If none of these are available then a
less exposed corner will do, but the client will almost certainly need
some real privacy and a few moments to take in the information
which you are providing. Although you might wish, or even need, to
rush off to something else, keeping your client with you at this stage
is an enormously important part of advocacy and time must be
allocated for it.

As with a preliminary hearing, even if you have had a good deal of
time to explain everything to the client and to answer any questions
at the hearing itself, you must follow up the hearing by reporting
fully to the client in writing what has occurred. Where you have had
a chance for some discussion with the client you can add to this
report any fruits of such a discussion, such as the client's agreement
to a particular course of resultant action. For solicitors the client

care rule 15 probably means that such behaviour is an expected form of good conduct.

8.5 IN THE COURT OFFICE

It may also be necessary to pay a visit to another section of the court office before you leave the courthouse. It is always useful to remember this possibility, because it can enormously speed whatever process is necessary, such as writing up the judgment, enforcing the judgment, preparing the appeal etc. Even where some element of procedure can be effected through correspondence, it can still be quite helpful if you have shown your face at the court office previously. It can then be easier to carry out the necessary procedure, once the wheels have been oiled and the court officials understand the issue more clearly and are able to recognise the human face of this case rather than simply its action number.

Before you leave, you should therefore pause to see whether there is anything further which needs to be done in the court office.

8.6 CONCLUSION

All of these mopping-up operations are extremely important in ensuring the fullest possible effects of your advocacy. You must be not simply a performer in the courtroom itself but also with your client and outside the court as well. Proper preparation will ensure that you will have considered most of these issues in advance. You need also to remember them after the heat of the action.

Conclusion

This book is intended as an introduction to the skills of advocacy. It is founded on the belief that there are certain basic elements of those skills which can be taught and understood and even put down on paper. The book also contains the elements of some exercises and a course for introducing new advocates to the practice of some of the behavioural skills mentioned.

As with all skills, theory and practice can only be brought together through proper experience. Such experience, if it is to be used for its proper educational value, must be carefully selected in an appropriate fashion. It is sensible to begin with shorter appearances, say, before masters of the High Court or district judges on pre-trial reviews before moving forward to a full-blown hearing or trial. This is partly because no book could expose the full intricacies and richness of real life and partly because each individual reacts differently to learning from developing experience.

Experience also, if it is to be used wisely, needs to be monitored. If unmonitored, experience can be a very bad teacher and practice will certainly not make perfect. This means that new advocates should be watched, at least on occasion, and rehearsed by those who supervise and train them. This monitoring should even occur sometimes in court or tribunal, because behaviour can change whilst carrying out the real task.

Criticism of behaviour is always difficult and should certainly be given only in a restrained form. The objective is to build up the new advocate's confidence, rather than to knock it down. Video replay of role playing can help also the behavioural aspects of performance, but is not essential; and the camera sometimes concentrates on elements not otherwise obvious.

The advocate can also pick up many cues and clues to behaviour by watching for the reactions of other participants in the courtroom. These will often tell you a great deal about how well you are doing and how well you are perceived. But do not rely entirely on the non-verbal behaviour of experienced judges who may well have learned to control some of their reactions. Do listen to any of the words or advice they or your opponents are prepared to give after your performance.

Learning from experience also involves proper time for considering what lessons need to be learned from each event. In the hurly-burly of practice life it is often difficult to set aside the time for a retrospective or post-mortem. But whether you have won or lost it is essential to realise what went well and what did not go quite so well in order to ensure that good forms of behaviour are repeated and bad forms of behaviour are not. Analysis of what occurred also provides a richer source of future inspiration. The reflective practitioner does more than simply tell 'war stories', pub jokes or dinner party routines. The objective of reflection is to bring together results that will inform the future.

Learning the behavioural skills addressed in this book will not necessarily be easy for all. Be prepared to make some mistakes and sometimes to fail. If you do not do so, you may never know why it is that you are getting it right. However, try to make your mistakes in preparation and role play rather than at the expense of your clients.

Above all — good luck!

Bibliography

Bergman, Paul, *Trial Advocacy in a Nutshell* (USA: West Publishing Co., 1979).

Bergman, Sherr and Burridge, *Games Law Teachers Play*. The Law Teacher.

Bergman, Sherr and Burridge, *Non-legally Specific Role Play*. Journal of Legal Education.

Evans, Keith, *Advocacy at the Bar: A Beginner's Guide* (London: Blackstone Press, 1983).

Sherr, Avrom, *Client Interviewing for Lawyers* (London: Sweet & Maxwell, 1986).

Sherr, Avrom, and Moorhead, Richard, and Paterson, Alan, *Transaction Criteria* (London: HMSO, 1992).